You Can Say "No" And Your Child Will Still Love You

Norma Ross, Ph.D.

Coauthored by Jason Eric Ross, M.S.Ed

Illustrations by Youzell Jeffers

Published by
Smart Parenting Solutions

Library of Congress Control Number: 2001117826
Ross, Norma,
You Can Say No And Your Child Will Still Love You

ISBN No. 0-9707451-0-9

Published by Smart Parenting Solutions
http://www.smartparentingsolutions.com

Acknowledgments

This book is dedicated to all the moms who came to my office in their quest to become better parents. I thank them all for making this book possible. It is also dedicated to all the wonderful kids from ages four to twenty-four who came to negotiate their bed-times, allowances, privileges and their responsibilities. I thank all the dads who came to give support to their wives. I hope the visits to my office helped them as well.

I want to thank my children, Jason and Lara, for their constant devotion to this project, their love, patience and of course, their computer lessons. I love them and I am so proud of both of them.

A special thanks goes to Howard Canaan and Stacy Quint for their editing advice. Thanks to Edward Jackowski for his constant motivation, and to David Levin for his direction.

Thanks to Youzell Jeffers from Nevis for designing the cover of the book. As he and I sat in my office in St. Kitts, I watched as he brought the cover to life from a pencil drawing. His considerable talent put the final touch on this project.

Contents

Prologue

So, after all, what is a parent?

A parent can play many roles. A parent can be a friend, a referee, a coach, a teacher, a confidant, a taskmaster or a disciplinarian. As a parent, I know that I have assumed all of these roles and I am sure you have also. The joy of seeing your child thrive is unlike anything else in the world. The effort you put forth may be endless and all consuming, and the emotions you feel will run from anger to frustration to realization and to bliss. Those emotions may be felt all in one day.

Preface — From a Parent to a Parent

I write this book in a position to view parenting from many different perspectives. I am the parent of two adult children and all indications are that they are happy and successful. I was a single parent for the latter part of my children's teenage years, after the loss of their father. I am a working mother who has had a twenty-year career as a parenting consultant. In those twenty years I have worked with hundreds of families to improve their relationships and have helped them deal with their everyday problems.

I began to take notes on my thoughts, observations, anecdotes and my experiences. I had no specific plan in mind for a book, but as I started to write, I realized that a blueprint was emerging. This blueprint was to help families get to a healthful place and highlighted what I believe are the fundamentals of parenting. It was the first time that I was able to see my guidance and advice to my clients and their families take form on paper. A formula emerged. It is practical and quite simple, and I believe it is too close and obvious for us to realize. I feel that parenting is really quite simple and instinctual, yet we get so far away from it because we are actually trying too hard. The truth is that we as parents can take control of our families and raise healthy, happy children if we look at parenting from a different perspective. This book is an attempt to bring the sum total of my experience and expertise by providing a plan that will make your journey as a parent easier and more successful. If you are concerned about how to deal with your children, let me assure you that you are not alone. I hope you will recognize aspects of yourself and your children in these pages.

As parents, we must realize that the pace and nature of our life are changing every day. Nowhere is this more evident than in watching our children grow up and seeing what they are exposed to. As a parenting consultant whose work consists of helping parents and their kids find ways to resolve interpersonal conflicts and problems, I have seen how the changing ways in which kids are socialized today affect them and their parents. This book is designed to help you navigate today's difficult world of child rearing. It will present you with a plan for parenting— a plan that has worked with the countless families I have worked with. I call it my blueprint for parenting.

Parenting is an **emotionally charged** endeavor, and our emotions often get in the way of our decision-making and better judgment. Parents need to eliminate what doesn't work, keep what's working well, and always look to improve things with new ideas and solutions. By helping you as a parent to better understand what you are going through, this book will empower you to handle your own emotions and your children's, and, by doing so, regain control of your family.

This is a practical book for parents who are busier than ever and need to discuss the here and now. After reading this book, you will have greater insight into why your children behave the way they do, but more important, how to prevent certain problems from arising before your child is grown. You will learn to say "no" to your children, and you will understand how and why to do so. It is all about learning to distinguish what is a reasonable request and what is not. You will learn how to be creative in communicating and modeling positive behaviors for your child. Lastly, you will understand the importance of feelings and the role they play in the parent-child relationship. The end result will be that your relationships with your children will flourish and you will have less stress, making you a better, more confident parent.

Parents always make mistakes. Our parents made mistakes and we survived. We will make mistakes and our children will survive. We're human. Making mistakes doesn't make us "bad" parents. If you understand that you can be wrong, your children can then also understand that they can be wrong. If you follow the principles of my parenting plan, you will be well on your way to developing and maintaining a happy, healthy family. At the same time, to be successful with this plan, parents need to apply it in thoughtful, creative and open-minded ways. This book will show you how. Remember that there is no perfect parent or child, so expect some difficulty along the way.

Let this book be your road map to building a successful family, no matter what your age, occupation, whether you are married, divorced or a single parent. The message is universal: ***In today's ever-changing world we need to take control of our children and our families.*** Only by doing this can we prepare our children for the world they face: schools, friends, siblings, the workplace, relationships, and eventually, their own family.

Kids Today Feel Empowered

In too many households today it is the kids, not the parents, who decide what to buy, where to go with friends, how late to stay out and make many more of the decisions that parents used to make. How did so many children gain this control? Often, we feel it is easier to give in to our children's demands, even though in our hearts, we know we shouldn't. Instead of confronting our children's demands and feelings of anger, we give in and by doing this, we set into motion a process that empowers our children. As time goes on, our children gain too much power. We then get angry with them for not wanting to give up the power. To deal with this issue early on, we need to set limits and say "no" to unreasonable requests. The earlier we do this in our kids' lives, the better.

Kids Need to Know About Boundaries and Limits

Parenting styles have changed over the past few generations and parents today have less authority — and are more inclined to let kids have their own way. Our society and culture present our children a world of media and advertising that reinforces the message that kids can and should be able to satisfy their desires. The appealing images of kids as consumers and the negative images of parental and authority figures that the media present make it even more difficult for kids to accept boundaries. Given this situation, parents need to assert themselves and be the ones who set boundaries and limits for our children.

Parents Need to Say "No" to Their Kids

Parents today are simply afraid to say "no" to their children. What started with "yes" to one request has spiraled out of control. Children today are demanding and expect to hear "yes" to every request. I will teach you to distinguish between a reasonable request and one that is unreasonable. By giving in to demands we know are unreasonable or not in their best interest we will only encourage more and more of these demands and our kids will not learn what is reasonable. In order for your children to learn that "no" is part of life, you need to break the cycle and start saying "no". And yes, your children will still love you. I will help prepare you with suitable responses for the angry outcries you may hear from your kids after they hear a "no". We need to recognize that an "I hate you" or a "You're a mean mom" are natural responses that a parent can live through and not reasons for automatically giving in to their kids' demands. Establishing rules and boundaries will not prevent our kids from loving and respecting us!

Whether We Know It or Not, Parents Are Always Influencing Their Kids

Kids model their behavior after the behavior of their parents. This is a fact of life. Our words and actions must model the types of behavior that we want our children to follow. By exhibiting calmness and using our judgment about what we think is right for our children, we will reinforce the same mature attitudes in them. On the same note, if we lose control of our emotions in confrontational moments with our kids, we will encourage the same acting out on their part. As our actions and attitudes will inevitably shape our kids' actions and attitudes, it's essential to model appropriate positive behavior for our kids. The principle of modeling can be applied to every aspect of our lives: the way we speak, the way we eat, if we exercise, whether we drink or smoke, not just our attitudes and emotions.

Effective Parenting Means Listening and Communicating

Showing our kids boundaries and re-empowering ourselves as parents will work only if we are in touch with our feelings and our children's feelings. In order to relate to and understand our children we must communicate. Children start communicating from the moment they are born. They cry, they talk, sometimes it is not even verbal. Parents must learn to recognize these signs of communication and act on them as early as possible. A child who knows that their parent is there for them from an early age, will be more likely to continue dialogue throughout life. We need to communicate our thoughts, questions, concerns and feelings and keep the lines of communication open to them at every stage of their growth. This sharing of thoughts and feelings between parent and child as he/she grows and develops will create the trust so that kids can accept parental decisions — even if they disagree with them.

Feelings

Parents need to recognize that feelings, for both the parents and children, highly influence their words, actions and behaviors. It is my goal that parents begin to realize the significant role these feelings play. Sometimes this is difficult, because we as parents don't want to feel bad or to see our children suffer. We need to help our children express their feelings, and help them to understand them. It is just as important that we understand our feelings as well. Lastly, just because we feel a certain way, we don't necessarily have to act that way. Only by recognizing feelings and the role they play can we help ourselves and our children.

Learning Parenting Strategies Offers You Lifelong Benefits

You may have picked up this book to help you solve a particular problem you are having with your child or you may be feeling as if you have lost control of your child or your family and this book will provide immediate assistance, to your concerns. Equally important, I hope that as you embark on the parenting journey, my parenting plan will help you build a relationship of closeness and trust with your child that will continue for life. After dealing with the challenges of raising a child, you will reap the reward of building a lasting and loving bond and of being able to help your child as a parent, friend, and advisor as he/she continues into adulthood.

So enjoy your journey through this book and this guided tour through the complex experience of parenting that it offers.

The Evolution of Parenting

Parenting Today and the Controlling, Sophisticated Child

If you look closely around you in shopping malls, in restaurants, in toy stores, or anywhere else where you see parents and children interact, you've probably noticed that today's child is more demanding, more controlling, and sounds more like an adult than ever before. You've probably also noticed that parents consequently appear to be more stressed than ever in confronting this "new" breed of child. Shocked, we watch this endless arguing as parents try to make their case to their child like lawyer Johnny Cochran and his Dream Team before Judge Ito.

When we see a parent somewhere trying to deal with out-of-control behavior, we may think, "Why can't this parent handle her child?" or, "That's not how I would handle my child!" or, "That's certainly not how my parents handled me!" That's true; our parents didn't handle us this way. Today's parent is losing an uphill battle against a child who is wiser, more confident, often more obstinate, and has been exposed to far more than we were as kids. While many of us may have difficulty finding the ON button for the computer, today's child uses the Internet with ease and skill.

Today's world is far different for children than it was for us. Children face tremendous pressures — getting into the right school or college, being popular, being thin, and being successful. They are more technologically savvy than we ever were.

They are more consumed with fitting in and being accepted by their peers. They look more to magazines and the media as their guides to what is important and acceptable. They demand more because there is so much more out there to ask for.

With their media sophistication and skill in manipulating modern technology, today's children are much better equipped to confront and control parents than in earlier generations. Children today decide where the family eats, what the family eats, where the family vacation is, what to buy, what to watch on TV, what time they go to bed and even whose voice is on the answering machine representing the family. If this trend continues, they'll soon be making our investment decisions and managing our investment portfolios.

Children today typically behave with the confidence and sense of authority of autocrats. Their attitudes demonstrate that they really think they are smarter than their parents. If you, like many other parents, feel manipulated in any of the ways listed above, with no control of your child or children, welcome to the stressful world of modern parenting. The horrific rise in school shootings over the last few years is further disturbing evidence of the depths children can sink to without proper supervision and intervention. Teen drug use is up, with an earlier onset than ever. Today there are more obese children than ever. The fact that over the last twenty years, my practice has become inundated with parents who are unsure of how to handle everyday child-rearing situations is further evidence that far too many parents today feel they have lost control of their children, and are searching for answers.

For parents and children, the world has changed dramatically since we were kids. It's not necessarily worse, but it's certainly different. With so many new opportunities, yet so many new problems, today is, in the words of Charles Dickens, both "the best of times" and "the worst of times." Parents are different, and kids are different. The level of women's education and professional responsibility has increased dramatically. In 1950, 3,358,000 women had college degrees. In 1998 more than six times as many, 20,142,000, had college degrees. In 1970, 28.7% of all mothers with children under the age of six were working.

By 1990 this percentage had grown to 58.2%. Between 1983 and 1992, the number of women working in managerial and professional specialties increased by 5.1 million.
{Department of Labor}

These statistics make it clear that not only has the world changed, but also life in general has changed for women. Years ago, more women were home raising children. The family could manage on one income. Today, that's no longer possible for many families. Instead, both parents now work and have enormous financial pressures. As one example of this change, finding adequate childcare because both parents are in the work force has come to demand the attention of many families. Nannies and baby-sitters have become an important part of the family structure. Corporate America has recognized this need and many companies are providing day care in order to retain their employees.

The way of a parent is a difficult path, filled with self-doubt and worry about being a good parent. Often problems are simple and can be dealt with easily, or resolve themselves and go away with little effort. But often, small problems become large ones and we feel overwhelmed. Parents who come to my office for consultations are usually educated and hard working. They love their children but have come to a roadblock in their efforts. They come into my office to get new ideas. My role with them is to help them be creative with their children and to remind them that there are many ways to handle any situation, and to help them find solutions to issues of concern for them.

Parents get pushed beyond their limits. They are upset with their children for asking for so much. Then they are tested. How am I doing as a parent? Am I giving too little? Am I giving too much? Will my child develop an eating disorder, turn to drugs or alcohol, get involved in gangs, etc.?

As the mother of a thirty year-old son and a twenty-seven year-old daughter, I can assure you that one of the greatest responsibilities I took on as a parent was asking for professional help when I needed some. In today's complex world, though, simply being an adult doesn't prepare us for parenting. The Internet, for instance, has entered our living room and parents need to set limits on whom the child communicates with over the World Wide Web. This issue didn't exist when we were being brought up. Instead of being taught to be leery of strangers who offer us candy as when we were being brought up, our children need to be taught and warned about prospective child molesters on Web sites luring them with e-mails.

At this point, I trust that I've struck a serious chord with most of you. Despite all our educational tools and advances in teaching, there has been an unexpected rise in learning disabilities, emotional and behavior problems in school and at home. If our society is more educated than ever, why do we still have difficulties with the basics of parenting — setting limits, dealing with temper tantrums, and associated issues? There are various reasons for this situation.

- The increasing divorce rate has weakened stable parental role models for children.

- The dramatic increase in families with two working parents over the last generation has drastically reduced the time that mothers spend raising their children.

- A more permissive attitude toward discipline has increased the problems parents face by disengaging them from the process of disciplining their children. By the time that they sense this and actively try to intervene in shaping their child's behavior, it may be too late to do much about it.

- The continued growth of an affluent, consumption-oriented culture makes it ever harder to say "no" to children's increasing demands for toys, clothes, personal telephone lines, and the thousands of other goods and services that we (unconsciously) and the world of commercial enterprise (deliberately) have trained them from an early age to demand.

- Finally, as children absorb their values from exposure to television, films, the Internet, the constant barrage of messages from entertainment media and video advertising, rather than from their parents, it threatens to further undermine parental authority — if we allow it to.

The reasons why a child may behave poorly are often numerous and diverse. A sudden drop in school grades or a dramatic shift in behavior patterns, for instance, does not automatically mean a child is using drugs, though it can be a sign that this is happening. No matter, in today's world we need to work at finding reasons, rather than simply attacking unwanted behavior and saying it's wrong.

In essence we have empowered children without even knowing it, and when we want to assume the reins, they don't want to give them up. The child is often the boss these days. I hear parents telling me that they are afraid of angering the child. Why? Children are supposed to have their feelings, good and bad; that's how they become well-adjusted adults. Children need to learn to recognize yet control certain feelings, among them anger. If you work at a company and have a temper tantrum every time things don't go the way you want, should you expect to move swiftly up the corporate ladder? You know the answer to this question, and your child should as well.

"No! No! No!" We all know the word, but parents often feel that they should never say "no" to their children. Why in the world not? "No" is the one word that they will hear in the real world for the rest of their lives, and parents need to prepare their children for it! Saying "no" is one of the most important elements of the parenting plan this book will present to you.

How My Interest in Parenting Began

My personal parenting plan began to develop in 1973 after I attended a lecture given by Dr. Hyman Spotnitz entitled, "The Role of the Father." Dr. Spotnitz is a noted psychoanalyst. At the time I was a mother of one child and was expecting my second, so the idea of having my husband actively involved in the parenting process was particularly appealing to me. As I sat in the audience, which was comprised of seasoned analysts, I realized that I was among one of the younger members of the group and that I was embarking on a journey that most in the room had already completed. As the impeccably dressed Dr. Spotnitz lectured, the proverbial light bulb went off in my head. What he said fit; it made sense and I was hooked. Raising a reasonable child — what a concept! As someone with a degree in business (I wasn't yet a therapist, analyst or counselor), this made sense to my business mind because it was about planning and getting results. That lecture, which I thought I was attending for the edification of my husband, turned out to be the most influential and eye-opening experience of my life. It guided me in how I raised my children, and eventually led me into the parent counseling that I now do professionally. Dr. Spotnitz served as my mentor throughout that journey and continues to be a valued advisor and teacher to me.

I learned a number of things that day:

- *The role of the father is to support the mother.*

- *A happy mother leads to happy children.*

- *The way to raise a reasonable child is to say yes to reasonable requests and no to unreasonable ones.*

- *Parents should address issues regarding their children in a united fashion. If they are in disagreement, they should address disagreements behind closed doors, not in front of their children.*

- *The way to teach children how to deal with their frustration is to permit or say yes to some of their requests and teach them that there will be a next time, and they will not get everything they want when they want it.*

- *Parents should keep their word and promises to their children.*

With these basics I raised my two children. They seem relatively happy and well adjusted now as young adults, so I know I've done all right. I also became a psychoanalyst whose practice now includes counseling individuals, couples, parents, children, and all types of families. My specialty has become parenting issues — assisting parents with the basic dilemmas they face every day with their children. This developed out of the recurring requests from clients for direction and guidance in parenting. The one common theme I observed with parents, and therefore the one that I opened this chapter with, is their simple inability to say "no" to their children. They have all the best intentions and for the most part have unlimited resources, but they simply can't get control of their children. By empowering them to say no to their children and explaining that their children will still love them, I've helped them to regain control of their families.

Parents everywhere are experiencing the same confusion and frustration about how to deal with the demands of children. For years we have indulged our children by saying "yes" to **every** request and whim. Now, when we try to say "no" our children cannot accept this as an answer. One hundred years ago children were exploited in factories and sweatshops; today children have so much authority that their parents feel powerless. How did this power shift come about? How have children been so misdirected or misguided that schools now require prison security systems and metal detectors for firearms? The following will show you how history has helped to affect the state of parenting today.

Parenting during the Great Depression

To better understand how and why parent-child relationships have changed, we need to begin around 1929, the beginning of the Great Depression. America had just experienced approximately a decade of prosperity after being victorious in World War I. As the names "The Jazz Age" and "The Roaring Twenties" suggest, during this decade, society for the most part reacted against the austerity of the Great War and was involved in a big party. Economically, politically and socially, people were relatively satisfied. Even Prohibition couldn't dampen this spirit of celebration that continued for more than ten years after the First World War. Yet during that time, traditional parental authority still prevailed. Children were "to be seen and not heard." They were expected to obey the Second Commandment and honor their father and mother and basically adhere to the roles defined for them by generations before them. The disciples of Freud and the founders of the sciences of psychology and psychiatry were just beginning to explore the possible negative effects of child rearing styles on the attitudes and behaviors of children when they become adults, but the results of their work had not yet had much of an impact on family life. By and large, parents still raised their children according to traditional authoritarian models.

Then the Depression hit. Families were devastated and many found themselves destitute. Farms and businesses failed. Fear was rampant throughout all segments of society (as President Franklin Roosevelt later recognized in the famous words of his 1933 Inaugural Address: "We have nothing to fear but fear itself").

For most people in the United States, financial security became not just a desire, but also a desperate necessity. People literally did not know where their next meal was coming from. The humiliation of standing on bread lines, eating in soup kitchens, selling apples on street corners, and futilely looking for work made for embittered adults, particularly men, in the 1930s. Through no fault of their own, men, previously cast in the roles of breadwinner and provider, were now failing at these tasks. Whether they were to blame or not, the results of America's economic collapse were that they were not living up to their self-perceived obligations. This sense of failure shaped their attitudes and behavior. They developed, for the most part, a fear-based approach to life that manifested itself in a "survival of the fittest" style of interpersonal relationships. Everyone was a prospective competitor, and the goal was to win, because winning meant your family could eat, and sleep where it was warm and dry. Emotional displays, or nurturing, as we see today, were perceived as behaviors that made one weak. Weakness meant failure, and failure could mean death, or, even worse in many minds, destitution. So parents during the Depression transmitted these attitudes to their children, offering by example the idea that parenting meant hardening children. Under the guise of protecting their children, parents during the Depression forced their children to ignore their emotions, and the emotions of others, and to achieve at all costs.

World War II: the Decline of Parental Nurturing

Just as America was coming out of the Depression, World War II started. Indeed, the economic boom brought about by the war helped to end the Depression. The United States went on a wartime footing officially after the attack on Pearl Harbor in 1941, but the nation had been reaping the economic benefits of the war in Europe since 1939 as a result of the Lend Lease Program and other government programs that increased manufacturing and trade with America's European allies before her entry into the war. Now there were jobs to be had everywhere. The Selective Service brought about the draft and millions of men were out of the work force and in the U.S. Army. Women were trained to take their place on the home front and also entered the work force in large numbers in what used to be considered "male" positions. Women were now factory workers and heavy machinery operators. The image of "Rosie the Riveter" building ships for the Navy was prevalent during the war.

World War II dramatically changed the dynamics of the family. With so many dads out of the house, all the parenting responsibilities fell on Mom, and she was now working, as well. With their father away and their mothers away from the house at work, children were left to their own resources. During the war years, as in the Depression years, children were encouraged to be tough, to hold feelings in and be emotionally undemonstrative. It's reasonable to assume that these factors, along with the overall effects of combat and exposure to the horrors of the Holocaust, on the collective psyche of American men served to reinforce the unemotional and reserved attitude that had been the main lesson taught by the Depression experience.

The '50s and New Suburban Lifestyle

The Depression and the Second World War however did not dampen in the slightest bit the propensity of American parents to produce children. The baby boom began as soon as the men returned home from the war. By the '50s children were being born at a remarkable rate, perhaps because of the relief married couples felt that they had survived both war and the Depression, and now wanted to raise families. Affluence had returned to postwar America, and the move to the suburbs was on. Parents were now able to provide financial security for themselves and their families. In politics and family life, the overall political climate of the times was conservative. As the war economy shifted to the production of consumer goods, parents began to indulge their children with more material possessions. Clothes, cars, the recently invented television, and other material things became more accessible to teenagers. More children were able to attend college. Children were becoming better educated and worldlier as parents tried to ensure that their children would not suffer the same deprivations that they had. Limits continued to be stretched, as parents became more indulgent, but still emotionally uninvolved with their children. The emotional and psychological needs of children continued to be ignored or discounted as parents continued to express of the non-nurturing behaviors and attitudes which had been used as survival skills during hard times.

The Rebellious '60s

Then the tumultuous sixties happened when an entire generation of young people, reacting to what they perceived as the failure of their parents and society in general to address their needs, rebelled against the status quo and insisted on making their feelings and demands heard. Among these rebellions were the civil rights movement, the peace movement, and the beginning of the feminist movement. The gap between parent and child, however, widened. Parents reacted either by becoming even more indulgent and failing to enforce any boundaries or limits on their children's behavior or by remaining inflexible and demanding that their children adhere to the attitudes and behaviors which they as children had been forced to conform to. Whatever parenting style they chose, with no models of nurturing, understanding parental communication in their backgrounds, parents in the sixties were poorly prepared for the challenges of child rearing that they faced.

The '70s and '80s: the New Breed of Parent

By the seventies and eighties this group of rebellious teenagers came of age and began having families of their own. As they became parents, this generation rapidly shifted from the "sex, drugs and rock n' roll" lifestyle to a materialistic one. One indication of this shift in values was that by the 1980s a degree in business administration had become the preferred degree for college students. In the '80s we also witnessed a significant increase in the number of women entering the full-time work force. Families required two salaries in order to maintain the materialistic lifestyle to which they aspired.

This created new problems in child rearing as the practicalities of life reduced the amount of time parents could spend with children. "Latchkey" children — children coming home from school to home with no one there — were becoming a widespread phenomenon. As they attempted to develop parenting skills, these new parents continued to experience the memories of alienation, misunderstanding and the absence of positive affection from their own childhood.

I surmise that the parents who were children in the '60s reacted to the lack of nurturing and affection that they received from their parents and now wanted to ensure that their children would never experience similar feelings of alienation. To make up for the more strained emotional bonding to their own parents, this new generation of parents wanted, and on some level felt they needed, the love and approval of their children. They vowed that their children would never react toward them with the negative feelings they had had for their parents. As a result, they indulged their children with whatever they felt had been denied to them, and, unlike their parents, they had the financial and economic wherewithal to do this. In an attempt to produce happy, functional families, the indulgence of parents which had begun to flower in the 1950s and had been rejected by the children in the rebellious 1960s was now back with a vengeance. We are seeing the unhealthful results of this indulgence today.

Three Simple Ways to Become a Better Parent Overnight

Communication

It is my hope that as you develop your plan for parenting, you will sit down with your child or children and begin a dialogue, which will continue for as long as you are in the role of parent. **Communication is crucial to every aspect of family life.** Remember, this process begins before our children are verbal, as our facial expressions and body language immediately set the tone for the child for better or for worse. Whether you have one child or ten children, whether you are a mother or a father, single, divorced or widowed, working or not, communication is essential to your quest for a healthful relationship with your children.

To be effective at raising children, parents need to communicate with each other as well, and the sooner this process is in place in a couple's relationship the better. Parents need to be in sync with each other and united about the philosophy of parenting they are about to embark on. Communication between spouses sets the whole tone for the parent-child relationship. If expectant parents develop their plan for parenting before the arrival of the child, they will almost intuitively find solutions for situations and concerns that baffle unprepared parents.

I continually see parents and children in public places where, more often than not, it is the parents disagreeing with each other. How can we effectively control our children if our children see us fighting as parents? If you already have children, you will likely see a marked improvement in behaviors and attitudes of all family members when communication becomes a priority. If you spend quality time with your children, take the time to talk to them and get to know what they are thinking and feeling; parenting will be not only easier, but also more enjoyable. Here are the basic principles of communication to follow to lay the foundation for successful parenting. Remember, your children need to know what is expected of them, and also what your input/responsibilities will be.

PRINCIPLES OF COMMUNICATION

- Always listen to your child's feelings.
- Always ask your child how their day was/always ask questions so you'll know what's going on.
- Always acknowledge your child's feelings and validate them as well, letting the child know you understand how they feel (even if you don't agree with them).
- Always compliment your child's positive behaviors (i.e., good grades, acting responsibly).
- Always try to offer solutions to your child's issues/problems.
- Always say YES to reasonable requests from your child.
- Always say NO to unreasonable requests (those that involve unsafe activities, financial burdens, dangerous behaviors).

The reality of the situation is that it is often difficult for parents to adhere to these principles. Parents are reactive and not proactive. When a problem arises, the parent questions him/herself, thinking "How did this happen? Where have I been?" Only then do we realize that we have not been communicating with our children for some time. Again, communication should begin well before your child is able to actually engage in dialogue or even speak. There needs to be a constant dialogue. Further, the parent who understands his/her own emotions and feelings is better equipped to understand the child's.

Buying our children toys, clothes, cars and cell phones is not an effective substitute for good communication. Talking to our children only when there is a problem is not communication, either. They are simply band-aid solutions at best. Real communication means talking to our children on a daily basis to understand what they are experiencing. Often parents find themselves so out of touch with their children that buying them material possessions is the only way they know how to connect with them. Communication is not about buying them things. It is not only being there for them, or paying attention to them for an afternoon, or attending one of their games or school events, but also having them know we are there for them as they travel through their emotional lives. Make time to talk to your children, ask questions and be a part of their life early on. This kind of communication, and the resulting trust it will encourage, should be your goal. Later, they will want to keep you involved. If you talk with your children when times are good, then you will be able to talk with them when times are bad. However, if you do not communicate early, it will be unreasonable for you to expect your child to come to you with their concerns later in life.

What a gift to children if, when they reach their teenage years, they have someone they trust implicitly, someone who — they can talk to about sexuality, careers, peer pressure, drugs and the myriad other problems they will face as they grow up. What a joy when that someone they trust is you!

It is essential that parents understand that it is up to us to develop a contract with our children right from the start that makes it clear that we are there for them even if there are disagreements and even if we do not see things in the same way. The important message that must be communicated to our children is that we are always here to listen, even if the hurt or feelings expressed by our kids may not appear that important in our minds.

We must realize that our children are small, and if they have a feeling we do not understand, it does not mean it is unimportant or any less real and important to them. If they can't get sympathy and understanding from us, they will look elsewhere for it. If our children always get the message that their parents don't understand them or respect their feelings, if they don't feel validated or understood by the parent, they will find peers that do. Peer pressure only wins out over parental influence when children don't feel comfortable going to parents. They reject the option of communicating with their parents and turn to their peers for advice or support. Those who don't turn to their peers may simply internalize their feelings.

There are many warning signs that your child may be internalizing their feelings. A child may begin to overeat, or stop eating, they may have difficulty concentrating in school and their grades may start to fall. With proper preparation, and having a plan, often we minimize the chance of seeing problems get out of control. Children grow up facing more jealousy, ridicule and hurt than ever. We should be on the lookout and try to listen and help them feel secure and safe.

Good communication has more to do with listening and being calm and has less to do with talking. Most parents report their sincere desire to get their children to talk rather than scream. Well, think of when and why anyone screams. People scream when they feel a desperate need to be heard and feel that no one is listening. A child who feels that nobody is listening to his or her needs and feelings responds the same way. We must make listening to them a priority.

When a child cries, he or she is communicating. When a child screams or has a temper tantrum, that child is unquestionably communicating. One of the most common mistakes parents make is to yell when a child cries or to scream back at a screaming child. Sometimes, a parent will even hit a crying child. These reactions are expressions of frustration, but are not productive responses.

These expressions communicate to the child that the parent is out of control. They do nothing to improve the behavior that the child is exhibiting, and often exacerbate the problem. Instead, a parent's goal should be to learn to recognize the child's cries as a form of communication and learn how to communicate back so that he/she feels understood.

Until the child can speak, parents need to take time to figure out what he/she is trying to communicate. The parent who stays in control and calmly deals with their child's behavior will be able to quickly take control of the situation. If the parent isn't patient in trying to figure out the child's needs and starts yelling, the child will sense this frustration and end up even more upset. Parents need to stay calm, cool, collected and focused so that they can respond in a positive way. Picking up a crying child, feeding a child, or talking, singing or making soothing sounds to a child are all examples of positive responses. By staying in control, parents model the behavior that they want their child to identify with, and in the end, that's the goal.

Besides talking with our children, playing with them and just sitting with them 'hanging out' are other methods of communication. Children tell me that they wish that sometimes their parents would just sit with them while they do their homework. This is not an outlandish or unreasonable request.

We mistakenly think that the more we talk to the child, the better off the child will be. **Listening** to children is as important, if not more important than talking to them. Just being there physically can be reassuring. As a parent, by listening to your child's feelings of unhappiness or hurt, as intense as they may be, you take a large step toward cementing the relationship with that child. Telling a child that you can see that they are hurt or sad is preferable to telling them they should not have that feeling. By listening to and letting the child talk about what he/she is feeling, you will help give the child confidence that you can help her or him resolve these feelings. If you can't tolerate your child's feelings, then prepare for a lot of heartache!

Don't deny them a very important lesson that life teaches: People can feel bad and still survive. The world won't end when they feel bad, and they won't feel bad forever.

A parent's goal in listening and keeping lines of communication open is for children to come to that parent first and often when there is a problem and to continue to do so throughout their developing years. Sure, there are going to be times when it is difficult for parents to listen to their children, just as it is often difficult for children to listen to their parents. Parents have difficulty listening to a child who is unhappy or angry or sad. As loving parents, we want to take any negative feeling away — and fast! So we often react impulsively, as children do, and try to take their bad feelings away or "fix" them. We tell our children that they "should not feel that way" or that "their feelings are wrong" or "they should be grateful for what they have." This response just further convinces children that they aren't being heard, which teaches them not to bother the next time they have a problem. So, what is truly important? Is it a feeling of being understood or getting some new toy or article of clothing? After all, are material possessions the heart and soul of the parent-child bond? Is it buying a toy that a child wants, or is it defined by the mere fact that the child knows their parents love them? Is it a feeling of security that children experience when they know their feelings are being listened to and heard?

Children often come to my office telling me that their parent was too busy to hear how terrible their day was, or that someone told them they were fat and the advice from the parents was to just ignore the insult. Love is more than telling the child to look away and not let critical or insulting remarks bother them. It is holding your child when he/she is feeling pain, asking how a hurtful remark made the child feel, or asking if he/she is ready to address the issue of being overweight, if that happens to be the problem. The child can at that point possibly discuss the fact that he/she needs some help.

Love means letting your child know that you are going to come up with ideas and that everyone is going to work together to make his or her life better. When a child feels hope, the child feels loved. Love is redefining what we need to give our children, and among the most important things are communicating and listening to feelings. They need those things that no sum of money can buy — the things of the heart.

Modeling

Modeling is a nonverbal form of communication. It consists of the behaviors that parents display, sometimes consciously, but more often unconsciously, to their children. We do not realize that we are constantly modeling for our children, for better or for worse. Often it is behavior that is second nature to us and we do not even know that we are doing it, such as yelling or cursing when we are frustrated. If it is second nature to us then it becomes a way of life for our children.

PRINCIPLES OF MODELING

- Always stay calm when addressing your child, because the child can sense when you are out of control.
- Do not react to your child; respond.
- Stick to the issues at hand, **not** the child's attitude.
- If you stay in shape and exercise and eat in moderation and model these habits for your child, the child is more likely to mimic them than by just being told what to do. You need to set the example.
- Children sense your positive and negative behaviors like radar at NASA, so always exhibit more of the good ones.

Modeling is perhaps the most effective form of communication we have, since it occurs even when we are not conscious of it. Our children observe everything that we do, even if we think they are not. They hear and mimic our language, our mannerisms and habits, both good and bad. It is important that parents model proper behavior for their children. An even temper, for instance, is one behavior pattern that parents can model for children of all ages. If your child has a temper tantrum and you stay calm, you are modeling good behavior. If your child is older and tries to upset you or get your attention by slamming doors or rolling his or her eyes, and you don't react to that, you are also modeling good behavior. When the parent is in control the child can sense it and this helps them learn how to calm down and control their own emotions.

The reverse also holds true: Children imitate negative behavior patterns, even if parents don't want them to. Telling a child, "Do what I say, not what I do" just doesn't work. A parent cannot teach honesty when he is stealing from his business. A parent cannot teach a child to eat healthily if he/she is constantly snacking on junk food. A parent who abuses drugs or alcohol cannot teach his or her child moderation. If parents model positive behavior, their children are more likely to mimic that behavior. If parents model negative behavior, their children will certainly imitate it. Children observe everything!

Modeling Healthy Lifestyles

One significant example of modeling is the way we care for ourselves. We model positive behavior when we take care of ourselves and eat properly, stay fit, and exercise. The message to the child is that we can take care of ourselves and they can do the same. Parents who lead a life of moderation teach their children that they too can lead a healthful life. We want our children to feel good about themselves. We can give them a sense of pride in how they look and how they feel by feeling good ourselves and by taking good care of ourselves.

Children who feel good about who they are can say "no" to drugs or alcohol and will not feel the need to starve themselves to "look good." They will already have that positive image of themselves.

Children are always watching and observing parental behavior, even when parents think they are not. Couple this with the media's constant barrage of "thin" images in the media, magazines constantly emphasizing the importance of being thin by presenting images of models as examples of what we should all look like. Is it any wonder that so many children today have distorted body images? We need to be strong as parents, and as people to be great role models for our kids.

Some children are starving themselves to look thin. Some are on diets when they are seven or eight. Other kids, feeling guilty about being fat, internalize their feelings and punish themselves by continuing to overeat. Either way, children are preoccupied with the way they look instead of just being kids. One sign of this condition is that when children at schools are asked about what health issue they feel is important, they talk about being thin rather than about finding a cure for diseases. Like it or not, this is where the world is today, at least in the United States.

To provide effective models for children's behavior, parents need healthful, realistic images of who they are and what they want to be. They need to model balance and moderation in everything they do. The parent who is in control can help the child who feels this hopelessness and loss of control to gain some. A parent who sees his or her child gaining weight can discuss the problem with the child while also modeling positive behavior. Of course, it would be ideal if the parent ate well, exercised regularly and gave the child the feeling that taking care of oneself is very important and should become second nature. When this happens, children may begin to walk or jog with their parents, or take up some other active sport or recreation, thus enabling them to have a better self-image.

Modeling Proper Values

Children who see their parents working hard, taking care of themselves, espousing good values, leading lives full of good deeds, and helping others will learn how to do the same. They will become the people that they see modeled in front of them. How can children learn values and to be forthright if they see their parents lying or cheating or not being responsible? Parents often do not realize or acknowledge that their children watch and see everything that they do.

As parents, we sometimes forget how important it is to teach children the basic value of being "a nice person." We should stop our child when he/she is hurtful to another child. Often parents stand aside and watch; they don't intervene and may even think the child's behavior is "cute." Parents may feel too embarrassed or may fear intervening. Such failure to intervene communicates the message to the child that this kind of behavior is acceptable, when it is not. The parent's silence is a cue for the child to continue this kind of aggressive or inappropriate behavior. If, as parents, we see a child making fun of another, it's tempting to dismiss this by saying to ourselves, or to each other, "Oh well, boys will be boys." Wrong! Boys will become, as will girls, what is modeled for them.

Children look to their parents for examples of how they should carry themselves in the world as men and women. For instance, if they see their father help with the household chores, they will learn that healthful relationships are partnerships. If they see doors being held, and amenities followed, if they hear the words "please" and "thank you" spoken, they will learn how to treat others and will expect to be treated with respect as well. If they see their parents supporting each other, respecting each other, recognizing each other's worth and dignity they will learn how healthful relationships are formed and maintained. All of this can be taught simply by modeling.

Modeling isn't limited to the aforementioned behaviors; it goes on all the time, in everything we do. When we treat our own parents well, our children are watching. When we give charity to the needy or talk about our concerns about others, we are modeling. When we remain calm when our child is having a tantrum, we are modeling. When we see our teenager's frustration and anger at us but remain calm, we are modeling. When we demand respectful behavior of children toward their parents and act respectfully toward our own, or others who are older, we are modeling. When a husband treats his wife with respect and supports her decisions, he is modeling good behavior for his son. When a wife treats her husband in the same cooperative manner, she is modeling good behavior for her daughter. When we remind our children about respecting their teachers, we are modeling by giving them a message about what is expected of them. If we light up a cigarette, how can we expect our children to do anything but that? If we drink too much, what message are we sending our children?

Kids today are very aware; they know when parents are doing the right thing. By communicating and modeling effectively, we can help our children make good decisions. I'm not saying that we have to be perfect as parents, but if we are sensitive to the influences that besiege our children and can listen to them, we can establish a trusting relationship with them. If we show moderation and control in our lives, we can help our children find the same kind of peace and comfort with themselves.

Don't Forget Feelings

Why is it so difficult to handle certain feelings? Both feelings we as parent's experience, and those that our children display or express can be so hard for us to handle.

We must realize that feelings are a part of life. Just as we breathe air or talk — we feel. It is part of the human condition. Many times we do not know what to do with our feelings.

Many of us choose negative, destructive behaviors as our way of dealing with how we feel or warding off how we feel. These behaviors can include overeating, using drugs and alcohol, smoking, acting out sexually and others. It is very easy to feel happy but feeling sad, hurt, angry, afraid or guilty can be a challenge.

Kids also have feelings all the time. Just because they are young doesn't mean they are not emotional. They experience many of the same feelings we do, just for different reasons. Often kids try to tell their parents how they are feeling. For example, a child might say, "I feel stupid in school," or "I feel fat when I look at other kids." Parents sometimes respond in a manner that attempts to change the feeling or take it away saying something such as, "You are not stupid" or "You are not fat, you look wonderful."

The problem with this approach is that it doesn't work and it doesn't work because it doesn't address the problem. The issue is not what the parent thinks; the issue is what the kid feels. By simply saying, "You are not stupid or fat" the parent will neither change how the child feels nor help the child address the feelings. The parent just does not want the child to feel badly — it is just a natural feeling. We want our kids never to suffer. The reality is that they hear "You are fat" or "You are stupid." They are faced with feelings of not being smart enough or that friends have more than they have. I hear these thoughts in my office all day long.

Recently, Allison, eleven years old, and her mother, came into my office. Allison recounted an incident that had occurred in school that day when a classmate, a boy, told her, "You know why you can't read very well? It's because you have too much blubber on your face!" She walked into my office visibly upset and unable to speak. I asked her, "How did that make you feel?" she said, "I felt horrible, absolutely horrible." I asked her, "What did you do?" She said, "I didn't do anything, I just walked away." I said to her, "I know you feel bad Allison, but I think you have to learn to respond to things like this in a positive way."

I suggested that the next time this young man said something to her that she just roll her eyes and tell him, "You're such a jerk" and then walk away.

Allison, her mother and I all laughed for a minute and Allison said she liked that idea. Allison spent several minutes practicing her response with her mother and me coaching her along. She left the office happy, and anxious to get back to school to try out her plan. She felt that we had helped her with a plan rather than telling her to ignore the boy. It was hard for Allison's mom to hear her daughter so sad but the reality was that life is full of words that are said to be hurtful and telling her to ignore the words was not working. Coming up with a plan just fit. Mom, of course, wants to help her child feel happy all the time. This does not always work. Allison needed to feel sad and then working on a plan of action made her feel as if she had some control.

Once again, in this example, the child's feelings were validated and she developed a plan of action that offered her hope. It's moments such as these that help a child and parent feel a closer connection to each other and give both a sense of hope. Most important of all, it confirms to the child that the parent is there for them, understands them, and is willing to help.

Now think about this.

Becky, your ten year-old is upset with your saying no to her request. She rolls her eyes, slams her door, and stays in her room. She is expressing a feeling. She cannot say how angry she feels so she is communicating her feelings through these behaviors. You as the parent think, "Boy does she have an attitude," and you believe that is the problem.

Overreacting to this would be unproductive; in fact, it could make the situation worse. First, and always, stay calm. Remember that she is simply expressing a feeling. In her own way she is having a temper tantrum that is somewhat appropriate to her age.

Respond calmly and let her be. She'll be back. When she returns you can address some issues, but the issues you address must be concrete, not attitudes. Yelling at her, telling her that she has an attitude accomplishes nothing. It neither helps her identify her feelings nor helps her in recognizing that some of her behavior might have been inappropriate. I suggest you let those comments go by and stick to concrete issues.

These issues include behaviors and setting boundaries for behaviors ("You can be as angry as you feel, but you cannot break anything in the house"), responsibilities ("I'm sorry you are angry but you know the rules, no TV until your homework is done"), or safety issues ("I appreciate that you are angry and I understand why but I think staying out till one a.m. at your age is dangerous and the answer is no")

When a parent finally gets to the point where they understand "attitude" in their child, it can be a wonderful moment, and a relief. Attitude is not a question — it is a statement. It is a communication from your child to you that they are unhappy with something you have done or said (usually hearing "no"), and that they think you don't know or understand what is going on. Later, after the child has calmed down you can address the communication, not the attitude.

Mothers come into my office with funny stories. We have a good time because there is nothing I haven't heard from others or experienced in my parenting career and the mothers feel understood and not quite so alone. Although we might laugh afterward, at the time it is very painful and difficult for them until they learn to make a parenting plan, and consistently follow it.

A teenager and their parents cannot go through these developmental years without getting upset, disappointed and angry. Parents need to communicate to their teenagers that there will be many times when they disagree, and that is okay. However, when it comes to health and safety issues the parent must consistently be the final decision maker based on the welfare of the child, even at the risk of the child's happiness. If a child knows that their reasonable requests are granted they can more easily accept a "no" when it involves an issue of health or safety.

Being Honest With Kids

Wanting to avoid painful feelings, ours and our children's, sometimes leads us to avoid being honest with them when honesty is what they need. To help them deal with certain problems, we need, in a tactful way, to **tell the truth**. Consider this situation, again based on the experiences of people whom I've worked with and have been able to help.

Sandy discussed with me how her son Brian came home from school one day and told her that his classmates said he had a big tummy. When he asked her if this was true, she said no. I then asked Sandy, "Is Brian's tummy big?" She replied yes. I asked her why she told him it wasn't. She said, "I didn't want him to feel bad, since I was fat when I was a kid." I explained to her that she would be helping her son by telling him the truth.

"To do what's best for Brian, you need to separate your feelings from your judgment and help Brian recognize and deal with his eating problem, or his tummy will get even bigger." So Sandy went back, told Brian the truth — that his tummy was a little big — and also told him that she understood how he felt and that together they would work on how to help him to eat less. By limiting the number of cookies that he ate, Sandy helped Brian deal with the issue of his weight.

Notice that Sandy was influenced by her personal history (her memory of feeling bad about being overweight) in not wanting to help Brian face his problem honestly. The greatest influence on how we raise our children is our childhood experiences. To keep them from having the painful experiences we had or to give them things we felt we were unfairly deprived of, we often keep them from hearing the truth or from accepting necessary rules and boundaries.

We may have come away from our earlier years saying, "I'll never force my kids to go to bed at eight o'clock when my friends were outside having fun the way my mother did to me" or, "I'll never criticize my kids and hurt their feelings the way my father did to me." With these thoughts in mind, we enter parenthood and thus never say "no" to our own kids because we as children didn't like to hear our parents say "no."

Not telling the truth, whether to avoid embarrassment or to protect the feelings of our kids, makes it harder to explain our reasons for saying "no" to them.

Consider this scenario: David's son Jerry has performed very well in high school and because of his accelerated work will be graduating one year early and has been accepted at the college of his choice with a partial scholarship. David and his wife, Lorraine, are very proud of their son, and the three of them had talked about the possibility of sending Jerry to France for a month during the summer. Unfortunately, David had suffered unexpected business reverses in the previous months and the rest of the family's funds were needed to help pay for college tuition. David realized that he couldn't realistically afford the trip to France that he knew his son was expecting and would have to give him a much less expensive graduation gift.

David hated the idea of frankly explaining his financial difficulties to his son and appearing as a failure to him. Instead, he planned to justify his decision by telling Jerry that he feared for his safety, that he didn't think he would be happy traveling alone, and that he wanted him to save up some money over the summer to prepare him for the expense of college. Lorraine disagreed with this strategy and convinced her husband to tell Jerry the truth: that although he very much wanted to him to take this trip, unexpected financial losses made this unfeasible.

Jerry was at first very disappointed when told of his graduation gift (a spring weekend in New Orleans with two friends of his), but he accepted the situation... as he had to. His father's honest explanation of what forced him to make his decision was certainly a factor in helping Jerry accept the situation.

After you make your statement be prepared for your child to be upset and unhappy. It's okay that they are upset. You can explain, "I know you're upset but I have to look out for your best interests and sometimes that means saying no."

A young child who feels unhappy may turn to food, or tune out in front of the television. Children who are constantly eating may be stuffing their feelings down with food instead of talking about them. Parents need to be aware that children have many feelings. As parents become verbal, children can develop the ability to verbalize their feelings instead of having temper tantrums.

Now some parents ask, how do I present these issues to my child? It's really quite simple, assuming that the concerns are discussed when the parent is calm, and prepared to deal with the feelings expressed by the child.

For instance, saying to your daughter, "Becky, I love you. I want only the best for you and sometimes that means saying no or denying you something. You want things, I want things. Neither one of us is going to get everything we want. But we can come to some agreement that is okay with all of us. I know you want to be your own person, and be independent, and I really appreciate that, but sometimes I'm going to have to limit that and say no, especially when it comes to your health and safety. I don't expect you to like it, but I do expect you to do what I say, and I hope you would try to understand that my reasons for doing it are based on my love for you."

Telling any child, especially a teenager, "Do it because I said so," or "Because I'm the parent, that's why," simply enrages the child (and rightfully so I might add) and this conveys to the child the message that you are simply wielding your power as a parent and an adult, rather than showing any caring, concern or rationale thought toward your child. It is always preferable to acknowledge their feelings by starting what you have to say with something such as, "I know you really want this — and I love you but...." Then gently but firmly say "no" and set the limits.

Always remember, that if the parenting plan you have created, or are creating, includes the granting of reasonable requests, and saying "yes" as often as is healthy and safe, then when it comes time to set a limit and say "no" the child will be more accepting and understanding of the need for the "no." Many times parents say "no" when they can just as easily say "yes". They exercise their power rather than good sense. If a child asks for more allowance, or a later curfew, or to see a friend, if it is feasible and safe, what is wrong with saying "yes"? Saying "no" just for the sake of saying "no" makes no sense. Try to say "yes" as often as you can because there are going to be so many situations where you must say "no."

I think that our difficulty in saying "no" is directly motivated by our desire to be loved by our children and our intense wish that they be happy. We don't want them to be angry with us because we somehow interpret this as meaning that they don't love us. Yet, we get angry with our children all the time and never stop loving them. All children, especially teenagers, are going to be angry with their parents when they hear the word "no." It is all about letting them have their feelings, the positive and negative ones, and for us to be strong enough and prepared enough to deal with all of them.

The family is like a team: Cooperation makes it successful. Like any sports or business team, the family must work together to be successful. Families that cooperate and work together set the foundation for their children's ability to create and maintain healthy, happy families of their own.

The most important point to remember in this chapter is that in spite of all the outside influences on our children, parent's behavior remains the most important one. Parents who communicate and model proper behavior and recognize the importance of feelings will have a smoother parenting journey.

You Can Say "No" and Your Child Will Still Love You

In my years of consulting with parents, I've come across just about every possible domestic scenario. My clients come to me for many reasons; their children fight among themselves, they don't listen to the parents, they fight in school, and they perform poorly in school. They also come to me because their children drink, take drugs, are overweight, underweight, or are subject to other types of destructive or uncontrolled behavior. It's easier to blame the problem on a divorce or on a death or peer pressure than it is to address it at its roots... the home.

Most parents who consult with me are well-intentioned, caring individuals, who just want the best for their kids. Whether due to guilt, or from having been deprived of material comforts or emotional support as children, parents often end up overindulging their children to make up for their real or perceived deficiencies. I call this the "I want my kids to have everything that I didn't have" syndrome. I believe that many parents need practical strategies to avoid falling into this trap or to get out of it.

We need to anticipate the confrontations that inevitably develop while raising children. Parents need to develop a plan of action and communication before their child is old enough to verbalize his or her demands. This plan involves modeling appropriate behavior for them. It requires that parents understand feelings and the role they play in our actions for both parents and children alike. Lastly, this plan must include saying "no" to our children and to understand that saying no is part of parenting, part of life and yes, our children will still love us. This chapter will teach you why it is important to say "no" and why parents have trouble saying "no."

Lastly, it will teach you when to say "no" and how to say "no." By understanding the importance of "no," you will be able to regain or simply maintain control of your family. The earlier you can start to take this new perspective on parenting the easier and more enjoyable your parenting journey will be. Trying to say "no" after overindulging a child for years will prove about as effective as cleaning up the oil spill from the Exxon *Valdez* with a vacuum cleaner. My goal in this book is to give you guidelines and ideas for handling your children before problems arise. I want to help you permanently rethink the way you approach the child-rearing process.

In considering all the people who come through my office, it seems that many parents resist asking for help. Parents think that parenting is easy and should come as second nature. Parents who are successful in the workplace don't like to think about the possibility that they are inadequate in the home environment. Many parents feel they should be all knowing and become frightened when a problem comes up that they can't understand and solve. We are concerned about our children; we want them to be happy, to have everything and anything that they want. Yet in the end, we are frustrated when we find that our efforts to give everything to our child have produced a more demanding child. When we overindulge our children they control the family. This happens for many reasons and now it is time to take back the control.

Why Parents Need To Say "No"

The word "no" is part of life. Children need to hear and to understand it. They will face it throughout their lives, whether in the home, at school, with teachers, friends, in the work place and in their personal relationships and families. If they hear it early in life it will prepare them for the world ahead. By saying "no" you will set the stage for them for the rest of their life. Saying "no" teaches them that life is a two-way street. Saying "no" will teach them responsibility, compromise and what will be expected from them. Saying "no" does not have to be punitive or harsh. It is not a bad thing but actually a positive part of the education of our children.

Saying "No" and the Difference Between Reasonable and Unreasonable

Saying "no" and saying "yes" has to do with what is reasonable and what is unreasonable. By understanding the difference, you will know when to say "no" and when to say yes and you will have an easier time doing so. This will also help you teach your children the difference and help them distinguish, too. A child who hears "yes" to everything will more than likely be demanding and will expect to get everything in life. They will feel the world revolves around them and will likely have difficulty adapting to the real world, which is quite different. Children who always hear "yes" may lose motivation and may feel that they do not have to work hard. They will feel entitled to everything and want everything. It is a parent's job to distinguish what is reasonable and what is not and to impart this to their children.

Here is an example of where a parent needs to take charge and act on what she deems best for her child.

Debbie came to me asking how she could explain to her six-year-old son Danny that his grandfather, whom he was very attached to, had passed away. It is important that you know a little information about Danny and his temperament. (It is important that you also understand the temperament of your child, so you are best equipped to handle a situation when it arises.) Danny is an only child. He is talkative and highly intelligent. Danny, although only six, usually gets what he asks for. His parents are usually saying "yes", even when they know they should say "no". It is important that we as parents make the decisions, not our children. Your child may possess the language skills of an adult, but have not lived long enough to possess their wisdom.

Debbie first consulted with her clergyman, who felt that Danny could go to the funeral. She then came to me to get my advice on the situation. I supported the idea, and felt that it was appropriate for Danny to go to the funeral and join in the ceremony of mourning.

Then Debbie added that Danny also wanted to go the grave. "Why?" I asked her. "Did he think it was a trip to McDonald's?" She paused at first and then laughed when she realized that at age six, Danny didn't even know what a grave site was. Debbie agreed that she would say "no" to Danny's request, even if it meant making him feel bad for a while. As it turned out, Danny's wish to visit his grandfather's grave was only a passing impulse, and he readily accepted his mother's decision.

Debbie was quite right to rely on her judgment about visiting a gravesite and not on that of her son, who was still too young to understand what his wish actually involved. Although it may seem unimportant, the correct handling of young children's unreasonable demands sets a pattern for either future success or future difficulties in raising them.

Many parents today think that if they give their child everything, they are being good parents and their children will be happy and love them. As a result, we indulge our children's every whim. How many times have we bought our child something (said "yes" to their request, when we wanted to say "no") that they either didn't need or we couldn't afford, because one of their friends had one? Children now decide what they buy, what they watch on TV, when they go to bed, whose voice is on the answering machine, where and what the family eats, and where the family vacations. If this trend continues, they will soon be making the family's investment decisions and managing its stock and bond portfolio! What started with "yes" to one unreasonable request to keep a child "happy" has led to an avalanche of unreasonable requests. Once this happens, it is virtually impossible to say "no." This loss of control is a subtle, gradual process. We don't even realize it is happening, until we wake up one day and realize that we have lost our power and authority and our children now feel more empowered. It is important that parents communicate and jointly establish what is reasonable and what is not. What is reasonable for one family may be unreasonable for another.

Saying "No" Sets Boundaries

Along with distinguishing reasonable from unreasonable, saying "no" helps in **setting boundaries**, which is essential to regaining control as a parent. To understand this, let's look at some examples based on the experiences of parents I've helped as a family consultant (here and throughout, the actual names of people have been changed to protect their privacy). Consider the following situation, which almost any parent will confront with a young child.

Suzie is having a tantrum at the mall. She is demanding her second ice cream and she hasn't even eaten dinner. It may calm her down to say "yes" and give her the ice cream, but this is not the correct response. You need to say, "Suzie, I know you want another ice cream but the answer is no, you've had enough." Suzie will be upset and angry. You will feel frustrated and that you are a bad parent. You may think why is Sandy, your friend's daughter, behaving so well, while Suzie just wants more and more. In order to get control of the situation, you may need to take Suzie out of the mall, and that is perfectly OK. You need to be prepared for situations such as this one, and when they occur, you need to be confident in your own judgment and stick to it. You need to address your feelings, accept that your child will have his or hers, and then put all of your feeling aside and take control.

This typical young-child-at-the-mall conflict may seem easy to settle but only if you as a parent deal with it early in your child's life and accustom him or her to certain rules and boundaries. Once this happens, your child will come to recognize these boundaries as a part of your role as parent. It doesn't mean that he/she will like them or quietly agree to them, but at some level he/she will accept them and learn to live with them. On the other hand, the longer you delay maintaining control when you think it's necessary, the more you take what seems the easy way out by caving in and saying, "yes," and the harder it will be to take charge of your child's behavior when more serious situations arise.

Letting your four-year-old have an extra ice cream in the mall and constantly saying "yes" to unreasonable requests can eventually cause more problems when the stakes are higher involving cars, alcohol and money issues. Take care of the issues when the issues are small. Here is another example of setting boundaries.

Ashley, Pat's thirteen-year-old, stays home from school on Friday because she is sick. Friday night there is a party. Suddenly Ashley feels better and wants to go. Pat tells her that she can't; she is sick. Ashley responds, "You're not a doctor! You're ridiculous; I feel better now," and adds, "I'll be the only child not at the party." Ashley has basically told her mother that she's a bad mom. So now among all her other feelings, Pat is hurt.

She can't understand how her child can say such terrible things and feel that way about her. Should she change her mind and let Ashley go to the party? She does not want her to miss out on any social activity. There should be no negotiation in this situation. If your child is sick and can't go to school for that reason, she can't go to the party, either. You may have to feel hurt or like a bad parent for the night, or maybe for the weekend, but you will have to learn to tolerate that feeling of distress. It too, will pass; as parents, we can't possibly give our children everything they want.

As parents, we have to accept responsibility for directing our children, realizing that this usually won't please them. More and more, your children will question the decisions you make about them: whom they will play with, when their curfew is, what clothing they wear, or what things they buy. Even something as simple as going to the supermarket becomes a struggle for parents as children go through the aisles not asking for, but demanding every item they've seen on TV. We as parents have to expect this and we must be prepared. Our children must learn to hear us say "no." Only in this way can we prepare them for the world they will face.

Remember, it is your job to say "no" and you will be teaching your child valuable lessons when you do so. In addition to saying no to unreasonable requests, the decision to say no may depend on financial burdens or constraints, or it may pertain to the safety of your child. Later on in the book, you will see specific interventions for saying no which are specific to the age of your child.

The situations covered in this chapter result from being so devoted to our children that we try to prevent them from having uncomfortable feelings. As parents, we often have reacted so negatively to our overly strict upbringing that we end up on the complete other end of the spectrum, being permissive, indecisive and guilt ridden. My sense is that overly permissive child rearing is a far greater problem that overly strict child rearing, so this is what I've chosen to emphasize.

However, treating children tyrannically is not what I'm urging. Whatever decisions you reach about your children should, of course, be made with their interests in mind, too. Compassion, concern, willingness to listen, and honest discussion of differences and feelings are essential to a healthy parent-child relationship. Such a relationship calls for moderation, and it requires that we say "no" to unreasonable requests and "yes" to the reasonable ones. The solution is not to say "no" to all requests because we are in charge. It requires that we distinguish between reasonable and unreasonable quests and that we act on a consistent basis. We need to impart an explanation to our children too so that they learn, they grow and they understand. Again, this is where separating our decisions from our feelings comes in.

If we say "yes" or "no" to our children on the basis of whatever feelings possess us at the moment, our decisions will be arbitrary and irrational — and will seem so to our children. We need to present them with a stable, consistent model of a parent's role in guiding and, where necessary, stepping in to direct their behavior.

Sometimes we will say "no" and later realize that we weren't being fair or didn't look at the complete picture. If our child's request was reasonable, and afterward we realize this, we can change our mind. We will make mistakes; we are human. We can change our "no" to a "yes" if we feel we have reacted too harshly.

The key theme of this chapter, however, is that it is never too late to start saying "no." It is never too late to learn and to change our behavior, to know when we are letting our emotions make decisions for us, and to be firm and hold our ground when we think we are right about our child. We want the best for our children: to have our children feel loved and to love us, for them to be safe, healthy and happy. Our goals may be great, but our method of reaching them may need to change.

Why Parents Have Difficulty Saying "No"

Quite simply, we as parents can't tolerate the feeling that we're depriving or upsetting our children. We don't want our children to be unhappy or angry with us, so we say "yes" to them to avoid having unbearable feelings. This section is devoted to these painful feelings — distress, guilt, and hurt — and the dilemmas that a parent faces. By understanding why we say yes, and what feelings we are trying to avoid, you will find it easier to start saying "no".

We must learn to tolerate these feelings. This is called ownership, not of a new car or home, but of our uncomfortable feelings. It's about how to deal with the feelings that we have about ourselves as parents, and about out children, and ultimately about the feelings that our children will have as a result of our behavior toward them. It's also about being able to set rules for children and facing problems honestly with them. I want to empower you to have all your feelings, help your children have theirs, and help you regain control of your family.

Earlier I suggested various reasons why we as parents have lost control of our families. The increasing divorce rate has weakened stable parental role models for children. The dramatic increase in families with two working parents over the last generation has drastically reduced the time that mothers spend raising their children. Changes in the world we live in have led parents to a generally more permissive attitude towards disciplining children. The continued growth of an affluent, consumption-oriented culture makes it ever harder to say "no" to children's increasing demands for toys, clothes, personal cell phones, and the thousands of other goods and services they have been trained from birth to want. The ongoing explosion of entertainment, media and technology further threatens to undermine parental authority as children absorb their values from exposure to television, films, the Internet, the constant barrage of advertising rather than from their parents. There are plenty of social, cultural, economic or technological explanations for how we got to where we are today.

Instead of passively accepting these factors as forces we are helpless against, we as parents need to see ourselves as agents of change in our kids' lives. Various trends in our society may have resulted in our children having a sense of empowerment, but we as parents are still capable of asserting our legitimate power ...if we are willing to make the effort. We must acknowledge that there is a problem and that we are a part of it. We must additionally acknowledge that we need to change how we relate — or don't relate — to our kids. We must work toward regaining the influence on our children's behavior, whether they are three or seventeen. So many parents today have lost this strength. Let me outline the steps that this process involves:

OWNERSHIP OF FEELINGS

- Accept the fact that both you and your children will have uncomfortable feelings and that this is natural.
- Recognize that these feelings have influenced your actions in the past.
- Recognize, understand and own your distressful feelings.
- Distinguish your feelings from your actions so they don't get in the way of making what you think is the right decision about your child.
- Help your children to own **their** feelings.
- Help them separate these feelings from their actions.
- Be committed to change
- Never give up!

These strategies may not be easy to accept at first. As parents, we will have to deal with many feelings, one of which is to face the fact that a close relationship can bring us so many unpleasant emotions and internal conflicts, and it is often difficult to deal with these feelings. It is difficult to act in a way that goes against our gut feeling, even if this means doing what is best for our child. It is perhaps even more difficult to teach our children, especially at an age when they are so dominated by their feelings, to similarly distance their actions from them. If you persist, however, you will be able to change your behavior, feel comfortable doing so, and gain some control over your child's behavior. If you can utilize these strategies, you will be on the way toward creating a happier family.

Avoiding Bad Feelings, Guilt and Inadequacy

Parents need to accept ownership of their feelings, both the good ones and the bad ones. In the outside world, we must face frustrations and disappointment, and as parents, we need to prepare our children for these realities as they attend school, socialize, deal with sibling rivalry and, through these experiences, learn to face limits and boundaries. A parent is not just the biological producer of a child, but someone who educates, guides, loves, coaches and decides whether to say "yes" or "no" to a child. If children don't learn the meaning of the word "no" at home, they won't be able to tolerate it anywhere else. It is not just our right, but also our job as parents to say "no."

Your child is going to be unhappy when he/she hears "no." He/she will be frustrated and angry with you. He/she might even say, "I hate you." It is OK; this is part of being a parent, of creating boundaries and setting limits. One of the most important skills in being a successful parent is owning and accepting your feelings, especially the uncomfortable ones. By "owning" your feelings, I mean recognizing whatever feelings you have but being able to act appropriately without letting these feelings cloud your judgment. For instance, a mother who has just grounded her daughter for the weekend because of repeatedly being late for curfews might recognize that she feels bad about the punishment she's given her daughter. She may feel that her daughter will be left out yet she knows that she must say "no." Parents often refuse to confront these kinds of painful feelings when they say "yes" even though they know they should say "no." As parents, we must accept the fact that saying "no" may make us feel bad. It may mean that our child may be angry with us, but these are feelings that we have to have. It doesn't mean we should say yes.

Another feeling that may arise if we say "no" to our children is guilt. Guilt is one of the most powerful and unbearable feelings, so it's human nature that people in general try to avoid it. Given the conditions of life today, feelings of guilt are inevitable.

Parents today work long hours, and often both parents are away from home. We have nannies raising our children or we place our children in daycare. Working is a part of our lives, whether we are married or single parents, so we have less time to spend with our children. It is normal to feel guilty that we are unable to spend more time with our kids. Yet we try avoiding further feelings of guilt at any cost. So, when our children ask for something, even if we know the request is unreasonable, we may automatically say "yes." We don't want to feel bad, so we give in. Similarly, when there has been a divorce, when there is new baby and the older child is jealous or unhappy, or where there has been a death in the family, one or both parents may try to alleviate their guilt feelings by saying "yes" too often, to unreasonable or excessive requests of their children, whether for material possessions or something as simple as staying out late.

In situations like these, we have to learn to recognize our feelings of guilt instead of acting impulsively to remove them. We need to acknowledge our sense of guilt, feel it and own it, but just not act on it. We're not going to stop working because our child wants to spend more time with us. We're not going to deprive our new baby of the love and affection he/she needs to keep an older sibling from feeling jealous. We can't totally protect our children from the difficult realities of divorce or death by showering them with gifts or privileges. The fact that we feel guilty doesn't mean that we have to give in to our child's every wish. It's OK to say "no." Guilt is a distressful part of life, but we can't try to avoid it by saying "yes" all the time. Doing this just leads to more demands on the part of your child and ultimately to a place where no parent wants to go and to a feeling no parent ever wants to have — I CAN'T STAND MY CHILD — a feeling which is even more difficult to own!

Like most parents, I've been through this distressful feeling of guilt. When my daughter was growing up, I was working many evenings toward the goal of getting my career off the ground.

One day, she wanted to go to the mall with her friends, and I was opposed to this. She had told me recently that I worked too much and was never home at night like the other moms. I felt guilty anyway about working evenings, even before she brought the issue up. My heart told me to let her go so I wouldn't feel more guilt, but my head told me that she might not be safe alone with her friends in a mall. So I told her she couldn't go. I had to own my feeling of guilt and accept that my daughter would be upset and angry... and she was. It wasn't the first time, nor would it be the last. She rolled her eyes and stormed out of the room, but I knew that I loved my daughter and she loved me and that she would get over these feelings. I knew I did not feel she was safe at the mall with her friends and I also knew that I wasn't home as much as I wanted to be. I had to own it all. This is the thought process that I went through and that I want to share with you.

This story has a happy conclusion. I received encouraging support for my decision when a call came an hour later from my daughter's friend's father, thanking me for saying "no" so that he could say "no" too. The girls still went out together, just not at the mall. That's how life goes. Sometimes there will be mutually acceptable solutions to parent-child conflicts, and sometimes compromises can be worked out, but at other times, parents must stick to their positions and learn to deal with the distressful feelings — theirs and their children's — that develop. Parents must own their feelings and help their children own theirs.

Associated with the guilt when saying "no" are two other distressful feelings parents have but try to avoid at all costs (no pun intended): insecurity and inadequacy about whether they are good parents. While trying to excel in their working and personal lives and to ensure that their children love them, parents from all walks of life seem to question their own parenting ability, especially when they have to say "no." It seems that it's not enough to excel in the workplace or be better at parenting than our parents were; we want to be super parents and raise super children. These unrealistically high expectations only add to the pressures that parenting naturally involves.

One way that we determine whether we're good parents is by what we can give our children. We usually measure this in terms of what we couldn't get as children. We want our children to have everything we didn't have and more. We want them to be happy at all times, and so we spend a flood of money on our children. We fill their days with more activities and their lives with TVs, computers, video games and cars than they can handle. But is this for their good or just so we will feel more secure about ourselves as parents?

Saying "no," especially at first, only makes these feelings stronger and more distressful. It makes our children react angrily, and sassy words such as these come out of their mouths:

"You're not fair!"
"You're a bad Mom/Dad!"
"I wish I had Debbie's mom."
"I wish I lived at Joey's house.
"I hate you!"
"You don't understand me."
"You don't love me!"
"Bobby's parents got him the newest Delta Force game."
"Danny's parents allowed him to have a later curfew."

Thus, saying "no" to our children, along with the distressful responses that follow, hits an already sensitive spot for the parent and adds to his or her inner conflict. We are already questioning our own skills, and now our children's criticism make us question ourselves even more. So of course we say "yes" to our children; who wants to feel like a bad parent? In order to keep our children from feeling any distress, we avoid owning our feelings.

YES! They Will Still Love You!

Why is it that when we think of saying no, we associate it with something negative? Saying "no" does not necessarily mean punishment, or that your child has done something wrong. It does not have to be harsh or punitive or imply that you are mad or disappointed with your child.

We as parents say yes to so many of our children's requests, when we want to say no, just so that our children won't be mad, or sad or think we are not good parents. We are actually trying too hard to make them happy and in the end we are doing our children a disservice. No is good; it is ok. It is part of life.

How can I convince you that your children will love you even when you say no to them? The only way for you to see is to try. I admit that they may not be happy with you when they first when they hear "no". They may be mad, they may yell or argue or even cry when you say "no". It is ok, let them have their feelings. You may feel bad too and that's ok; you need to have your feelings, too. This is a part of life that you need to experience and accept in order to overcome. Life is full of many uncomfortable feelings. Your children may be angry, but they won't be mad or angry forever. It is temporary. Your child does not hate you, and they aren't going to run away or ask the neighbor to adopt them.

The most important part of saying no is to take the time to explain why you are saying no, and to explain to them the difference between reasonable and unreasonable requests, so they will have an easier time digesting it. If you say yes to what is reasonable then they will understand the difference and come to accept that you are the parent, that you set the rules and the boundaries. They will also see that you are fair. Believe it or not, your child knows when you are arbitrarily saying no and when you are saying it out of concern. They will understand that you are doing your job as a parent and that you are looking out for their welfare, for their safety and what is in their best interest. The more you can communicate this to your child the easier it will be for them to accept. With time you notice that your child is less reactive to the word *no.* Actually, if you always say yes to your child, your child will more than likely know that there are few boundaries and they will know they can get their way, and will probably have less respect for you for being submissive.

If your child can get accustomed to hearing both yes and no from an early age and they can understand why, then you will both have an easier time than you think. Children learn quickly; they will catch on. Remember that saying no does not have to be delivered in an angry tone or in a manner that is perceived as a punishment. If it is delivered calmly, with a short explanation, without any yelling, then it will be easier for them to accept and understand.

My Conclusion on Saying NO

Remember, it is your job to say no and you will be teaching your child valuable lessons when you do so. In addition to saying no to unreasonable requests, the decision to say "no" may depend on financial burdens or constraints, or it may pertain to the safety of your child. Again, later on in the book, you will see specific interventions for saying no which are specific to the age of your child.

Many parents today feel they have lost control of their children. Furthermore, they now feel anger, resentment and frustration with the child they have created. We've given our children everything we can afford, and in many cases, things we can't afford because it was easier than saying "no." We've filled every waking hour with activities from play-dates, to tennis, karate, music lessons and computers, just to make them happy. What do we get in return for having tried to give our child everything? A child who is demanding, spoiled, and unappreciative. A child who complains of being "bored" as soon as he/she has a free moment.

How different from my childhood! I grew up with one doll, a few books and my imagination, and I was never bored. After everything we have tried to do for our children, our greatest fear has come true: Our children are unhappy. Even worse, they may not even like us! This hurts, and it's only natural that we may feel sad, angry and/or frustrated with our children and our own parenting abilities.

Keep in mind that this is usually a gradual process that creeps up on us. It does not happen overnight. One day we wake up and find that our child is ordering us around, telling us what to do, what to buy and what to think. We may think, "How can this be my child, I tried to be a good parent and give my child everything, and now look what I have created."

Now it is your time to regain control. It will not happen overnight, but if you are dedicated to making a change and following a plan, you will get there, I promise. It takes admitting there is a problem and then committing to making a change. We the parent must take the first step even it if means feeling inadequate or having some uncomfortable feelings. There is nothing wrong in saying "no," and we have to be confident in our decision to do so. We can ease the parenting process by owning our feelings, understanding our children's and learning when to say "no" and when to say "yes."

Saying "no" is part of successful communication and therefore essential to successful parenting. This book will teach you how to create a bond with your child so you will be able to say "no," and — most important — *your child will still love you!*

The Toddler Years: "Winning is Everything!"

The Toddler Years: "Winning Is Everything!"

A Profile of the Toddler Years

After a child is a little past the first year, he/she has moved beyond babyhood and is becoming much more actively engaged with the surrounding world. This age is a time of rapid development. It marks the beginning of language formation, of curiosity about the surrounding world, and of asking "Why?" about everything. It's a period of intense physical activity as the toddler constantly touches, pushes, shoves and threatens to break things as he/she navigates an exciting new world of objects. It marks the beginning of bladder and elimination control. The toddler now strives for psychological autonomy, and along with this comes the beginning of negativism and resistance to parental authority. However the toddler experiences conflicted states: He/she wants independence, but at times he/she wants the comfort and security of being a baby.

Dealing With the Little Explorer

Children at this age are certainly curious, and they have no sense of safety or of the value of the things around them — and I mean **none**. A family heirloom is just as inviting as some inexpensive object within the child's reach. Placing his or her finger in the electric outlet or sticking his or her hand in a pot of boiling tomato sauce appears to be a great way to start the morning. Unfortunately, padding all the walls with rubber is not a solution. So parents need to "child-proof" their homes so that objects that they don't want damaged as well as anything that can cause injury or harm is kept out of their children's way. Besides protecting the child and the house, doing this reduces the number of times the necessity for a "no" arises so that "no" can be saved for addressing significant situations. This is the age of mobility, of touching, of exploring. By fifteen months, a child can now navigate without help and is curious about everything, because everything is new. The child reaches for things, bumps into things, and breaks things. At this toddler stage, children want everything, want to touch everything and don't have the capacity to know what is good for them. Soon they will become more aware of their limitations, but not yet. As the child discovers that this new and fascinating world doesn't always fit with his or her desires, this is also the age of tantrums. This is when a parent sees his or her child's first personality traits and behavior quirks. Some you will enjoy; others you will not. It should be clear why now is when the "no's" begin, for both parent and child. Now, not later in the child's life, is the time to create a parenting plan and put it into effect.

Remember, the "no's" must be well thought out and kept to a minimum. We want our children to be joyful and interested in all things. We want their personalities to flourish and their creativity to grow. We want them to experience new things and learn and explore. Children who hear "no" all the time can have their curiosity dampened and the healthy development of their personality can be affected. So it is incumbent on us as good, caring parents to keep the turmoil, which is a natural part of the toddler's behavior from upsetting us so much that we lose our tempers, and yell "no" to our child too often. Parents need to be prepared for the child's behavior and provide an environment where their children can be themselves yet learn how to navigate in a world that is competitive and difficult for them to understand.

Having a parenting plan is essential for getting through this difficult period with ease and creativity and without "losing it." Decide what you are going to say "no" to and what you are planning to do before your child is involving you in a hard-to-control situation.

Recognize but don't be overwhelmed by your anger or resentment; these are natural, understandable reactions, so tell yourself it is okay to have all of these feelings. Take comfort — passing through this stage successfully by applying the principles of the parenting plan will lead to more peace and less conflict in the following stages of your child's development.

Being Flexible With the Toddler

By the toddler age, you will have learned to understand your child's temperament and disposition. This will help you develop your parenting plan, as it needs to be adjusted for dealing with the temperaments of different children; an intense child with uncontrolled energy, for example, needs to be dealt with differently from a passive child. Comparing one sibling to another more passive one can be harmful. Each child is an individual, and difficult as a parent may find it to understand, two children from the same family can be as different as night and day. You need to factor the features of each child's temperament into your the plan of action, especially in the case of a child who wants to test and challenge all the time. **Do not get into constant battles.** Have a plan and stick to it as much as you can, but be flexible and creative at this important formative stage in your child's development as much as possible, in order not to stifle your child's personal growth by saying "no" too easily and too often.

One of the most important issues that parents need to keep in mind at this stage is that we want our children to feel good about themselves. So when you say "no" at this stage, don't tell the child in a way to suggest that he/she is bad for asking for things. Instead, show that you recognize your child's feelings by saying something such as:

- *I know you want everything.*
  or
- *I know that you cannot control yourself at times.*

The emphasis must be on modeling desired behavior, not on venting frustration. Toddlers are trying to learn what the world is offering, and if parents set limits while accepting who they are, they will feel that their desires are okay, even if they can't have what they want. In this way, their self-esteem will develop very early. Parents can't expect children to feel good about themselves if they constantly yell at them for their behavior. Tantrums, for instance, can't be rewarded, but a child who has tantrums shouldn't be threatened with loss of love or abandonment, either. If a child and parent develop a good bond, the tantrums will decrease.

Having a Consistent Plan

At the same time, a parent should try to be consistent. The toddler age is the stage the child begins to learn of the consistency and reliability of his/her parents. Parents who say "no" to something today and allow it tomorrow teach their child that whether or not behaviors are appropriate depends upon the whim or mood of the parent. For example, if mommy says "no" to her child's request when doing the laundry, but says "yes" to her child's request when she's on the phone, the child will learn to discriminate when he/she can get what he/she wants, and will likely use this knowledge to their advantage. These kinds of mixed messages can lead to serious problems in the later developmental stages of a child. Parents who don't remain consistent with and committed to their decisions concerning what is acceptable and reasonable and what deserves a "no" also teach their child that they can be manipulated. When the child finds this out, a tyrant is born. Once a parent consistently says "yes" to unreasonable requests, children continue to demand more and more, and this process accustoms them to making unreasonable demands. Children are quick learners, so a parent needs to be prepared with a plan about what it is reasonable and what it is unreasonable to say "yes" to.

Parents often ask, "How do I know what is reasonable?" My response is always, "You know!" A gut feeling never lies. Trust your experience, your intuition, and your common sense. Let's take a practical situation. It's dinnertime, and James now wants cookies and ice cream and does not want to eat dinner. His mother, Anne, says, "James, it's dinnertime and mommy will let you have two cookies after dinner. Mom knows that you like cookies but in our house, we eat dinner first."

She is calm because she has a plan, and part of the plan is to say "yes" to reasonable requests. Anne is firm; she doesn't use too many words, and if a tantrum comes, she is prepared to say to James, "I will be in the kitchen, so when you are ready to be calm, you know where to find me." This is her plan; she is going to stick to it, even if a part of her is feeling, "I am a bad mother" or "He will be angry at me." She tries to stay calm, with no yelling or raised voices. If she is prepared, she will stay focused, knowing that she is not giving in; no matter how difficult James may get, she will remain in emotional control.

On the other hand, if James wears his mother down and she gives in, he has discovered that a tantrum has gotten him the results he wants — cookies before dinner. If this happens, no one wins. James will get the cookies, Anne will become upset at herself and at James, and a pattern will have been set in motion. Gradually Anne will come to feel unhappy with her son and start wondering how on earth this feeling ever developed. Meanwhile, James' demands will escalate until they become totally unreasonable. The parent will have started on the long, slippery slope down the road to total loss of control.

Modeling Behavior for the Toddler

Cindy and Matthew are another mother and child who have gone through typical toddler issues. I've worked in my office with Cindy at developing a plan for dealing with Matthew when he tries to manipulate her. One day, for instance, Matthew was playing with another boy, Jay, and took the toy Jay was playing with. Cindy got upset with Matthew but realized that pushing and shoving are part of his stage of development. At the same time, she doesn't want her son to hit other children, so she decided that she would deal with the important issue of Matthew's behavior with a plan, and that led to the following conversation:

Cindy: *Matthew, we just do not hit other children; it is not acceptable.*

Matthew: *I want my toy.*

Cindy: *I know you wanted the toy, but you have to ask Jay or mommy for it. We just do not hit. It's not acceptable and mommy is not happy when you hit. Mommy will always help you if you ask for help.*

Cindy knows that toddlers hit; they still need to learn that words are more appropriate ways of getting what they want. Cindy didn't want Matthew to feel guilty or that he was a bad person, but she did want to focus on a behavior of his that could lead to a problem.

If Cindy herself hits Matthew when she is frustrated, then the dialogue would change:

Cindy: *Matthew, hitting is not permitted. I know mommy has hit you, but mommy is not going to hit and Matthew is not going to hit. We are both going to use our words when we are angry. Okay?*

Cindy has now learned that when she hits Matthew, she is unintentionally modeling behavior so that Matthew will also be inclined to hit when he is angry. So instead, she is going to model how she wants Matthew to put his feelings of anger or frustration into words.

For parent and child, the toddler years are a time of learning about each other. I like to compare a parent who has raised a child for a while to the president of a company who knows his product inside out. Cindy is now becoming aware of her product, Matthew. She is learning about him — who he is, what works in dealing with him, and what does not. She is also learning about herself and what makes her "tick", and so is Matthew. Even if he doesn't yet understand that he should not hit, he senses that mom is not happy with him. Her voice is firm. He will get the message, as well as the reassurance that she still loves him.

Having a Plan for Bedtime

Bedtime is another situation where having a plan is important. Cindy is putting Matthew to bed, and he wants her to sit with him. This is a reasonable request, and spending time with Matthew at bedtime is part of her new plan, even if Cindy is tired at the end of the day. He may have had a hard day, also. So for now, Cindy is just comforting Matthew, sitting next to him or reading one book. If she is too tired, then dad can sit with Matthew.

Now the question is, how long do they sit with him? Knowing Matthew, they already can tell that they may have to put a time limit to this request. Matthew will probably want ten books but that is unreasonable and also overstimulating.

So Cindy and Matthew's dad, Dave, discuss how they are going to handle this issue. They agree that they are going to limit the reading to two books, even if Matthew gets upset. When Dave goes in to read to him, he sets the limits straight away by saying: "Matthew, daddy is excited about reading **two** books to you before bed." Sure enough, after the second book, Matthew starts pushing — he wants another book read to him. Dave explains that there will be only two books, but he will sit with Matthew and there will be no more talking because now it is quiet time. Dad is tired, but not too tired that he will change the agreed upon plan. He knows that Matthew has a hard time when he doesn't get his way and that there needs to be a quiet moment before bedtime. Even though Matthew is trying to manipulate him, Dave calmly tells him, "Daddy knows you want more books but now is the time to go to sleep. Dad will sit with you quietly. Dad loves you." Dave's calm attitude will help Matthew. It is part of the modeling behavior for Matthew that Dave and Cindy plan to use in order to raise a reasonable child. If Dave screams at Matthew to go to bed, then Matthew will start to scream back, and this doesn't help anyone.

A toddler needs a quiet moment so he/she can leave the exciting world he/she is becoming aware of. Toddlers don't want to miss anything, and often they can become overstimulated in the evening. The father who comes home late often wants to play with the toddler. When he is finished playing, he thinks his child should also be ready to stop, but toddlers don't yet understand this. They want to keep playing while parents want to put them to bed. This can be an area of conflict because a young child just wants to have fun, dad just wanted to feel like he was a good father, and now mom is exasperated because the child she has been dealing with since daybreak doesn't want to end his or her day. So within Cindy's new plan, she and Dave have decided that play at night will not be overstimulating. Dad will take his cues from Cindy, and they will be aware of making nighttime more peaceful without too many "no" words.

Two Powerful Weapons: "No's" and Tantrums

The most dramatic manifestation of the toddler stage is the development of the child's negativism or resistance to doing what parents wish. This is normal and essential to his or her development. Just as parents (I hope) are using the word "no," the child learns it and begins to use it, usually against them, to test boundaries and limits and to exercise power. The more frantic a parent becomes and the more frustration he/she exhibits at hearing the child say "no," the more the child realizes just how powerful that word is. Defiance, the child discovers, can get what he/she wants. If used successfully — and a parent can't always **deny** a child's wishes — "no" for the child is a very useful tool.

Children model our good behavior and also our inappropriate behavior. By remaining calm Cindy is giving Matthew a positive example to follow. She is also helping him put his feelings into words, an invaluable tool that will follow him through adulthood.

How often have we seen our children, and other children, having a temper tantrum while out shopping with their parents? Many times parents react to their child's tantrum as inappropriately as the child. This is due in large part to the parents' frustration and embarrassment, as well as their not being prepared for their child's behavior. Cindy and I discussed this specific issue of taking her toddler along while shopping. First I had to help her see the situation from Matthew's perspective. While she was shopping, there he was, being dragged around for several hours, doing nothing that is of any interest to him and having very little attention paid to him because mom is busy and focused on other things. Eventually, and inevitably, he is going to want to change the situation. The best way he knows how to do this is to have a tantrum. Given the circumstances, this behavior is perfectly understandable and should come as no surprise to Cindy when it does happen.

This type of situation can be prevented with some planning and foresight. The first alternative is not to take the child shopping or to a restaurant, or anywhere where a tantrum is likely to be precipitated. Leave the child home until he or she is old enough to handle such an outing; he/she will have plenty of opportunities to go shopping in the future.

I realize that sometimes parents need to go shopping with their toddlers, but if it's possible, leaving them with a friend can be more positive than taking them along, especially if you are constantly yelling at them and expecting them to exhibit anything approaching adult behavior. If you are willing to or need to take your toddler along, bring a toy or toys to engage their attention. At this age, children cannot be reasoned with, but they can be distracted. So if Cindy is creative and can find something to occupy Matthew's attention, that's great. Providing distractions for a child during a shopping or other trip can be a wonderfully effective tool at this age in helping the child control and engage him/herself. Have toys available for when you are shopping or in the car. The prepared parent will not leave home without them.

Lasty, the toddler years is the stage where children's control of their bladder and elimination begins. Depending on how toilet training is dealt with, the child can begin to have a period of either greater tension or greater ease. I don't think that toilet training should be an area of behavior where parents set rigid rules. A child will develop control in this area at his or own pace. Certainly, practicing at the potty should be encouraged at the right time, but common sense and restraint are better than demands or emotional abuse. The issue of elimination can be the beginning of other issues of control between parent and child, and making a crisis of it can set a negative pattern for the rest of the parent-child relationship. It's best for a parent to let the child's development take its natural course. The less anxiety the parent shows here, the less gets passed on to the child.

Taking Control and Staying Calm

Parents need to model calm behavior for the young child. When Matthew doesn't want to get into his car seat, his dad stays calm. Without yelling, he just picks Matthew up and puts him there. At this stage, when a child is just learning to verbalize, fewer words and more actions are called for. The child is not yet developmentally "ready" to truly conceptualize rationalizations and/or explanations. When Matthew jumps onto the furniture and mom is upset when he ignores her directive: "No, we do not jump on the furniture," Cindy just picks him up and distracts him. When Matthew is in the restaurant and wants to run around and cannot control himself, mom must take him out rather than expect him to listen. He may not understand the idea that a restaurant is a place where people eat and talk. This goes back to the preparation part of the plan. Parents should prepare the child in advance for the restaurant "experience," so the child has an idea of what to expect and how to behave when there. Parents need to understand what appropriate behavior at this stage consists of and what type of toddler they have. If they had one child who was a perfect angel in a restaurant and now they have a child who cannot sit for more than a minute, they must accept these different temperaments and realize the uniqueness of each child. It may sometimes be hard to accept, but parents may have to be creating an environment that is particularly geared to the child who is more difficult and is less reasonable than their other child or their best friend's child.

Dave and Cindy have worked on a plan suited for Matthew's particular temperament:

- *Prepare Matthew for* ***everything*** *— places he will visit, people he will meet, decisions you have made concerning him, etc.*
- *Don't take Matthew to places where he is likely to get out of control.*
- *Don't get Matthew overstimulated before bedtime.*
- *Don't read too many books to Matthew before bedtime.*
- *Make sure Matthew gets enough rest.*
- *Say "Yes" to Matthew's reasonable requests.*
- *Say "No" to his unreasonable requests.*
- *Keep in communication with each other about Matthew.*

Dave is supporting Cindy and this part of their plan. They are both trying to be consistent and create a world for Matthew in which he is able to touch, observe, learn, and, above all, feel good about himself. He will be able to tolerate the "no's" because Cindy and Dave understand who he is and what makes him behave as he does.

They understand that setting limits is part of a parent's job description. They also know that Matthew may try to manipulate them to get his way, but they are a team and Matthew knows that his parents are in charge and that he is secure in that world — and that is the way it should be.

Understanding the special features of the toddler stage and developing a plan to deal with them will set the pattern for your child's later development. "As the twig is bent, so grows the tree." The toddler can be a tease and can drive a parent to distraction, but such behavior is normal for this particular time in a child's life. Forbidden fruit can be very alluring at this age, so parents have to set firm and definitive limits while still giving the child enough flexibility to develop healthily. Parents need to feel comfortable with their decisions and treat the toddler with understanding but also with a plan. Parents who are tentative about saying "no" invite the child to test them more. Ignoring tantrums and keeping calm when the child is excited are ways to model behavior at this age.

The next chapter will follow kids, now at the preschool stage, where they will meet new issues.

Five Common Scenarios and Interventions for Saying "No" to Your Toddler

• Example 1

Your toddler is running around the table at dinner and won't calm down.

What you really want to say… "Can't you sit down, what is wrong with you?"

What you can say… "We all eat together; we do not run around during dinner." If you think the child can be calmed down have him sit on your lap, to distract him. If not, do not push against an immovable force. Remove the child from the dining environment completely. Yelling will accomplish nothing here.

• Example 2

Your toddler is sitting at a restaurant with other kids and moms who are calm and yours is not — obviously to your acute embarrassment.

What you really want to say… "Why can't you behave like the other kids?"

What you can do… Pick the child up and remove him from the table, bring him outside if possible. You can say, "No, Stephen, we do not behave this way in a restaurant." If the child cannot calm himself with your help or that of a distracting toy, you have to follow the logic in the previous example and leave.

• Example 3

Your toddler does not want to get into his car seat, and you are going on a long trip. There are no options here. The child does not win this time!

What you really want to do… You are probably at your wit's end and angry, perhaps ready to spank or strike the child.

What you can do… Grab your spouse (assuming you have one) to deal with the situation and diffuse it. Talking may not solve the problem here. If you have a spouse, your best option is to have one of you sit with the child.

• Example 4

Your toddler is hitting everyone in sight, including you. This is the biggest issue you will come across, because it pervades all environments.

• Example 5

Your toddler is in the bathroom and his bowel movements are all over the bathroom walls.

What you really want to say... . "What the hell is wrong with you? How can you be so stupid? Shame on you!!!"

What you can say ... "No, Stephen, I know you want to be an artist but not on the walls" — you then go out and get your child the necessary pads and crayons, etc. to show him the proper environment for his artistic expression (you should have these things on hand already)

What you really want to do... You want to hit the child and yell and scream at him.

What you can do... Take his arms and gently place them by his side and say, "We do not hit people. I do not hit you, and you are not to hit others!" Be stern and look directly into the child's eyes. Tell the child what he CAN hit! Punching bags are a great way for the child to diffuse his anger.

The Preschool Years: "Little Lawyers"

The Preschool Years: "Little Lawyers"

A Profile of the Preschooler

Once your child has reached age three, he/she is no longer a toddler and is now moving into what should be an easier stage for the parent. Your child probably has some mastery of language by now. He/she is now already in or preparing to be in some school setting where the teacher and friends reign and is in the process of forming attachments away from the parent. I hope, after perhaps experiencing some adjustment pains — the child loves his or her new environment and is bubbling over with ideas and requests. The child is working toward more maturity (by completing toilet training, for instance) and by age five he or she is quite the little person, with a distinctive and recognizable personality.

At this stage, you will see many exciting signs of your child's development. His or her language skills dramatically increase. The average four-year-old, for instance, asks questions all day long — a clear sign of his or her increasing self-awareness and awareness of the world. At this age children are still inconsistent in their behavior and their attitudes; becoming toilet trained, but still having "accidents," chattering uncontrollably at times and then giving one-word answers at others, acting sensitively at one moment and with cruelty the next. Your child will experience and express more varied and complex feelings. To some extent, these feelings may be turned inward or projected onto toys or fantasy figures. At the same time, he/she will begin to form attachments outside of the family with friends and teachers, part of an overall behavior shift from overdependence to independence.

Bedtime Issues and Impulsive Behavior

So how do we say no to the child who has now entered the world of being social? He/she doesn't want to miss out on any fun. Sometimes preschoolers just don't want to go to sleep, but at this stage they need a lot of structure. They should know that a certain time, let's say eight p.m., is their bedtime and that a story or two will be read. When they want four stories, as we saw in the previous chapter, you have to set a limit.

As with the number of stories read, your child's amount of physical activity before bed needs to be controlled. The demands to extend playtime when your child is already tired must be dealt with calmly. At this age, children do not really understand that taking a rest is an option to playing; it is the parent who needs to reinforce this point. The parent who is too unstructured and lets the child run the show at age four is about to set foot into dark, unmanageable territory. A four-year-old should not be telling the parent that he/she is the boss.

I remember the first time a pediatrician referred the mother of a four-year-old to me. This exasperated mom had been driven to screaming and even to physical action out of frustration at her daughter, Rebecca, who is quite verbal and wants everything she sees. When Rebecca came to my office with her mom, she appeared to be an adorable child who spoke beautifully and was happy to play with the toys that I gave her while I spoke to her mom, Carolyn.

She was well behaved until the end of the session when her mother was ready to go. At that point, she asked for another toy and her mother made the mistake of saying okay when she really needed to say, "Rebecca, we are ready to go now and there is no more playing." Rebecca was just trying to see if she was going to get her way — and she did. Carolyn just wanted to avoid saying "no." Instead, she needed to understand that Rebecca could not have everything she wanted and that at some point she had to say "no."

That's life — four-year-olds need limits. The preschooler's demands are the beginning of many demands. The parent has to be careful that they do not keep giving in just because the child speaks so well and is so articulate. Often times parents are so seduced by and impressed with a child's increasing verbal abilities that they tend to succumb to their unreasonable requests, while ignoring the disservice that they are doing to the child. The more a parent rewards the language, and subsequently ends up giving in to the unreasonable requests, the more empowered the child becomes. The more empowered the child becomes, the more they want and demand. While it is okay to praise their verbal prowess, we must be careful not to simultaneously reward their language in a way that meets their inappropriate demands. The no's will be a critical component at this stage — especially for demanding, verbal children such as Rebecca.

The purpose for the visit was for me to observe Rebecca. At first we talked about Rebecca's wanting to watch two videos before bedtime and about how she was unable to wind down after so much stimulation. I suggested that perhaps two videos were too much and that sitting with Rebecca after reading a book might be better. I tried to make the point that parents have to experiment with ideas and make decisions based on their understanding of their child's temperament and maturity. They need to understand that their child who is four and wants everything he/she can ask for is not the best person to make decisions. The preschooler, who may be bright, adorable and now verbal, needs no's whenever a request is unreasonable. At the preschool stage, with the child's increased verbal understanding, the parent is in a perfect position to begin saying yes to reasonable requests and no to unreasonable requests. In Rebecca's case, Carolyn, who thought two videos were reasonable, had to rethink her decision for next time after she found that her daughter could not fall asleep easily.

So Carolyn and I discussed the fact that parents are always in the process of rethinking decisions if something they thought was reasonable turns out not to be. The next time Rebecca requests two videos, Carolyn can say, " Mom thinks that a book before you go to sleep may be a better idea. So tonight we are going to read a book, and as a special treat mom will sit with you to help you go to sleep." This sets a pattern that mom or dad can follow; it also establishes bedtime as reading time and spending quiet time with Rebecca. This kind of routine will help Rebecca and her mom at the end of a day.

At this point, you may be asking, "What if I try this and my child throws a major tantrum at nine or ten in the evening? What do I do then?" Well, you have several choices:

- *You can sit there and say, "I'll wait until you calm down and behave."*

- *You can say, "I'll be back when you are calm," leave the room, and give your child a chance to calm down by him/herself.*

- *You can say, "If you can't stop crying, you will lose privileges this week. This is not the way we behave." (Of course, you need to be ready to carry out what you say about your child losing privileges if the tantrum doesn't stop.)*

If both parents are home, one should assist the other. Here, as always, when parents work as a team, they can respond to behavior issues much more easily. Whatever you decide to do, remember to **stay calm** no matter what.

At age four, Rebecca is someone who has trouble waiting, and we all have to know that this is part of her temperament. She needs to be helped with her impulsive behavior, although her parents were yelling at her when they came to my office initially. That is never a solution. We have worked at trying to change everyone's behavior, and slowly this is starting to happen.

The teacher communicates to Carolyn, then Carolyn tells me, and I then discuss some of the issues with Rebecca. Early in her visits to my office, Rebecca negotiated her rights and discussed her impulsive behavior. Then, on one visit, when asking mom for a lollipop, Rebecca could not wait. I asked Rebecca if it was too hard to wait, and she said yes. Then I told her quietly that she had to wait because the lollipop was in the car, and it would take time to get it. I told her I knew it was difficult, and I understood, but that screaming was not helping it be better. She sat on my sofa trying to stay in control. This was hard for her, especially when she saw her little sister with a pop. However, a moment later, her lollipop arrived. Without using loud words, I had helped her get her pop and learn how to wait.

Social and Sibling Issues

Rebecca is also now a social being with a social calendar. She has made new friends at school and constantly wants to play. Her mom now has to decide how many play-dates Rebecca should have, when, and with whom. Rebecca also has trouble leaving play-dates. She hates change, and she hates when playtime ends. As with bedtime play, Carolyn has to explain and set boundaries for Rebecca's activities.

One week Carolyn called me for some special help with Rebecca. Rebecca and her friend Melissa were playing at Melissa's house. The nanny was in the other room when the two four-year-olds decided to play with toy scissors, and Rebecca subsequently cut Melissa's hair. Carolyn called me frantically about the situation. "Had anyone gotten hurt?" I asked. After getting no for an answer, I followed up with a lighter question: "Did Rebecca do a good job?" Eventually Carolyn took things pretty well. She rushed to the haircutter with the two girls to even out the mess. That done, she told Rebecca that she was very upset with her behavior: "**No!** We do **not** touch scissors unless we ask permission. Scissors can be very dangerous, and they are not a toy." Carolyn then told

Rebecca that her behavior was totally unacceptable and that because of it there would be no TV that evening.

Carolyn expressed to me that she and her husband had been arguing the night before, and she thought this had upset Rebecca. So the next day Carolyn brought Rebecca to my office, and the discussion was not only humorous, but also dealt with serious issues and ended up being a teaching/learning experience. Here is how part of it went:

Norma: *Well, Rebecca, I hear that mom wasn't too happy yesterday.*

Rebecca: *I cut my friend's hair and mommy was not happy with me.*

Norma: *Do you understand that scissors are very dangerous?*

Rebecca: *Yes, I know I can hurt someone's eyes with them.*

Norma: *Do you think you should be punished for not listening to mom and playing with scissors?*

Rebecca: *Only if I do it again.*

Norma: *Do you think you understand what we are talking about?*

Rebecca*: Yes. I will not use scissors to cut hair until I am older or without permission or I cut hair like a job. They are not a toy.*
(Mom had talked about people cutting hair as a job.)

This "no" had blossomed into a learning experience. Rebecca was not yelled at or told she was horrible. She ended up in my office and we talked about not getting the special present that she was promised. She was upset; yet she spoke clearly and with the maturity of an older child. This doesn't mean that she was never going to behave inappropriately again, but Rebecca had been helped to understand that her mom and dad were not happy with her behavior and that they would keep watching her. She is a child with many impulses and does not have the ability to stop herself before she gets into trouble. So for now, she needs outside forces to help her with her impulse control.

Meanwhile, Carolyn, who also has an infant, has to make decisions involving both of her children now. Rebecca has to share, both at home and at school. She is on her best behavior at school, so she is now physically taking out her impulses at home on her sister. Her behavior with Amanda, who is twenty-two months old, is at a dangerous level. Her mom is worried about having to deal with Rebecca's anger at her sister for being cute and loving. She walks by Amanda and pushes and shoves her. Mom has yelled and screamed and now has to deal with two issues — Rebecca's impulsive, aggressive acting out, and her own lack of control when she sees Rebecca abusing her sister. She has to control herself and not react negatively to her four-year-old.

In a very calm way, Rebecca is told that pushing is not acceptable behavior. Mom tells her that she is unhappy with her behavior and it has to stop. When Rebecca screams, "I hate her," Carolyn stays calm and says, " You can hate her or be angry, but you cannot hit or push." Mom is validating Rebecca's feelings, but saying no to Rebecca's unacceptable behavior. Despite what she feels like doing, she is focused and modeling calm behavior for her daughter; she has told her four-year-old: "No, we do not behave this way." Rebecca is at a stage where she can understand. Now Carolyn can expect to hear from Rebecca about how terrible it is to have a sister and what a bad mom she is for having a new baby. She tries to be prepared for anything she is about to hear, but she is feeling overwhelmed. Rebecca is unhappy and totally out of control. The no's are now centered on safety for the sibling.

The most important breakthrough in handling Rebecca's behavior issues and her mother's emotional exhaustion was dad's visit to my office to offer emotional support for mom. This was a wonderful gift for Carolyn, who until then had to handle many issues alone. Dad has now taken over dealing with Rebecca's behavior toward Amanda. Whenever she pushes her younger sister, mom and now dad have the same approach. For the first time Rebecca sees dad in the picture, not yelling but calmly saying, "Rebecca, mom and dad are not happy when you hit your sister. Please go to your room right now. This behavior is not acceptable."

Rebecca has been used to her parents screaming; their new approach jolts her. She doesn't like the idea of not being daddy's girl anymore. Instead of hitting Rebecca or yelling that it is terrible to hit, mom and dad together are going to say, calmly and firmly, "No — this is not behavior we are going to accept." Previously Rebecca had gotten the message that **she** was bad, and that became a self-fulfilling prophecy. Now she is going to hear only about her **behavior**. Instead of getting a great deal of negative attention for her impulsivity, she is getting a short "Mom and dad are upset with your behavior." It is critical for parents to focus on the **actions** of the child, as opposed to the **actual** child; this will, in turn, encourage Rebecca to do the same. At the same time, Rebecca's positive acts are being complimented.

Just the notion that Carolyn feels supported by Rebecca's father has enabled both her and her husband to be more successful in their parenting endeavor. Of course having a place where she can vent and also get some new solutions has helped her self-confidence in the art of saying no. The storm is not over; this is just the first step, but there is a significant change in the air: Mom and dad are now united and supportive. No longer is dad yelling at mom for Rebecca's misdeeds. He is asking her what she needs to deal with the situation. They have also decided to have a code word when one of them is losing their cool. They are communicating with each other about Rebecca. This may sound simple, but believe me, it isn't. For parents to be united, they have to have a meeting of minds and a plan.

At the same time, there is no need to go to extremes over issue of contention with a child, especially issues that are not going to remain. For instance, Michael, five, was driving his mother Beryl crazy because he wanted to wear only sweat pants and not the jeans that she wanted him to wear. Beryl loves good-looking clothes for her kids, and Michael has a wardrobe of designer outfits. She kept fighting with him about the sweat pants until I advised her to give that battle up; it wasn't worth the irritation. Michael was in a loose clothing stage and would probably grow out of it. In any case, he wasn't going to walk down the wedding aisle in sweat pants. Certain battles rooted in parental longing for their child to look good are just not worth the fight. I told her to let it be, and for a while he had different sweats for every day of the week. Six months later, he was ready for his designer look, and his mother was ecstatic. Michael's request was a harmless request and, considering his age, a reasonable one.

Saying "No" to Aggressive Behavior

Mark is three and his mother, Nancy, gets a note from his teacher that he is pushing kids when he does not get his way. Nancy is in my office, mortified that her son is now having a behavior problem at the young age of three. Nancy and Mark's dad are extremely permissive with their only son, who is the center of their universe. For his parents, Mark can do no wrong, and they have set for him no limits. Now, because the school is not happy with Mark's behavior, mom and dad are going to have to start setting some.

Mark's mom and dad are in my office to establish a strategy for dealing with Mark. Mark will have to hear a no and a firm one: "We just do not push, in school or anywhere. Pushing can hurt others and can be very dangerous." If Mark has difficulty, then dad will have to take away some extra privileges until Mark displays some self-control. Mom and dad will have to say that they spoke to the teacher and they are unhappy with the news. At school the teacher is the boss and he will have to stop his pushing and hitting. Mom and dad and the teacher, who is now an important part of Mark's life, are going to talk to one another until Mark's behavior improves.

Mark will try to justify his behavior with his new language skills, but his parents have to be firm and stay focused on the message, "No, we just do not push when we are angry." Mark, who got his way at home for a long time, has to be helped with his behavior. He needs limits and even if this is preschool, it is a time where habits that are not healthful need immediate attention. Mark will be watched because he may need that help to curtail his aggressive behavior.

While saying "no" to the unreasonable requests mentioned thus far is important, aggressive behaviors such as Mark's warrant an immediate no-tolerance attitude — for safety issues, as well as social ones.

So the "No's" at the preschool stage take on a new form because children are now learning how to speak in a way that can be shocking. With their newfound language skills, they try new words and try to get what they want in any way they can — like little lawyers. Often parents let their children talk and talk because they sound so bright, and then the child takes over. Parents have to be cautious about giving children too much verbal power, even at the dinner table. Children need to learn to listen and give others a chance to speak, as well.

Parents need to remember that they can be dealing with a child who is so verbal that they don't realize how manipulative he/she is. Yes, a child who is "so cute and bright" can be a parent's pride and joy, but while enjoying their child's precociousness, parents need to be aware that the child who has now mastered language so much is now going to use these newfound language skills to try to get his parents to say "yes" all the time. The kid who is so wonderful at five and gets his way all the time will seem much less wonderful and much more emotionally draining when grade school age comes and there are so many more things for him to ask for and to debate with his parents about.

Let's follow your child as he/she is now ready for grade school.

Five Common Scenarios and Interventions for Saying "No" to Your Preschooler

• Example 1

Your preschooler is jumping on the sofa, near a glass table, a recipe for disaster!

What you really want to say... "Get off that sofa right now, don't you see the glass table?!"

What you can do... Walk up to the child immediately, grab him and pull him off and say, "This is dangerous. No, we do not jump on furniture anywhere." Find a place they can jump and begin explaining the appropriateness of certain behaviors and the consequences associated with them.

• Example 2

Your preschooler runs into the street!

What you really want to do... You want to yell, "DON'T EVER DO THAT AGAIN, YOU CAN GET KILLED!"

What you can say... The same thing. This time your gut is correct. The child should be scared, and even if you make him cry, you have conveyed beyond the shadow of a doubt how serious this is.

• **Example 3**

Your preschooler is becoming physical with you and others. You are at a stage where the word "no" may not stop the behavior, but you CAN explain to the child reasoning.

What you really want to say... (see toddler example 5)

What you can say... "No, we do not hit. You can be angry, but we do not hit. If you are angry with me you can tell me, but you are not allowed to hit!"
The child can understand the difference between having a feeling, and acting on it. You can now have a dialogue with your child because he can verbalize what he feels. You won't like what he has to say, but it beats getting punched.

• **Example 4**

Your preschooler is getting into trouble at school. He is pushing kids and trying to be at the front of the line for every activity and calling out of turn constantly. It appears as if he has no impulse control.

What you really want to say... it doesn't matter what you want to say —

What you can say and better do... Intervene, and speak to the teacher and really listen to what she has to say. Your child is undoubtedly upset about something, and is showing it... to everyone. It is not a stage! It may be the child's temperament and you need to make sure how to best deal with it. When speaking to the child, focus on the child's behavior. You need to have a form of discipline to help him with the impulse control. So if the child acts out, he cannot watch his favorite cartoons for a predetermined amount of time. This way the child understands that behaviors good and bad have consequences. The actions are bad and the child needs to know that. Telling him he is bad is harmful and counterproductive. Speak to your pediatrician as well.

• Example 5

Your preschooler wants to go to a friend's house after school. You know she is tired, since she just returned from a long trip. You want the child to go for social reasons, but know she needs rest.

What you really want to say... "Don't you know you're tired?"

What you can say... "Jennifer, I think you are tired, and you can go to your friend's this week." When she kicks and screams, pick her up, do not scream and say, "I love you and know you're tired, you need to rest. Let's see about visiting your friend tomorrow."

The Grade School Years
"Budding Teens"

The Grade School Years "Budding Teens"

A Profile of the Grade Schooler

At six, children are ready for school. They are toilet-trained, fluent and about to embark on a very special journey. Apart from their parents, school and friends will be the most important influences on their lives. The intense conflict of the toddler period has subsided. As the child's language skills and ability to really understand issues have developed, your life may become a bit easier. Kids now want to learn, play and absorb their new independence. They aspire to be teenagers. Often their aggression will be very visible, especially toward siblings. Moms and dads will now be faced with a new phase of life: They are needed when their child has a problem, but they will be pushed away for friends as part of their new quest for independence. They need to realize that this process of turning to peers and away from parents is a normal and healthy part of growth and should not be taken as a personal response to them.

The Media and Today's Grade Schooler

Being eight today is very different from what it was when we were eight. Today's eight-year-olds are more Internet savvy than their parents. They talk to their friends via computer as routinely as we pick up a phone (not that they don't use the phone too). Because of their access to the media, they know more about violence — at least indirectly — than we ever knew. They know about divorce, sex and health issues in a way that we could never have imagined. They learn about CD's, music and designer jeans before they are ten. They're less naive, less innocent, and more sophisticated than we ever were at their age.

They are skilled linguistic negotiators, which would keep us reeling with joy — if only those skills were left at school each day! When they negotiate and question parents constantly, parents become overwhelmed and are quick to react, rather than to respond. Subsequently, problems ensue. Proud of their growing sophistication, grade schoolers act like experts at everything.

Media advertising bombards them with appeals and images strictly geared to their wishes and fantasies. They want to fit in, to be "cool," to be popular. To fulfill these desires, they are faced with pressures that we couldn't have imagined as children. This is an age when moms are in my office discussing how much their children are asking just to be like everyone else. To be popular, they have to be thin, so they're forced to worry about their physical appearance earlier than we did. As some professionals would say, they're pressured to be more narcissistic, more concerned about their self-image than past generations were.

Our grade schoolers' world is a different one from ours, and parents have to understand it in order to deal with it. This age is important because it gives us the opportunity to teach and create a bond with our children while they are still quite responsive to our influence, a bond that will, we hope, last through the years no matter what pressures they face. Kids see everything on TV and ask for everything they see, and as a result parents spend a significant part of their time shopping for their children. This consumer environment is the world we live in, and we can't be angry with our kids for the world that we have created. We can, however, teach them moderation by saying "no" when they ask for something they do not need or we cannot afford. Teaching kids boundaries and setting up the lines of communication now when problems are relatively small helps build a strong foundation for whatever the future might bring. At this stage, bonds and goals are set, and values and morals are instilled.

Handling Internet Issues

The six to twelve-year-olds that I meet in my practice teach me about life in suburbia or in the big city. For instance, one mother, Sharon, was telling me in my office about walking in on Heather, age ten going on twenty, while Heather was on the Internet. Sharon was shocked to see something sexual on the screen, so she exploded and started screaming at Heather. While discussing the incident in my office, Sharon explained how upset she was with Heather. She was also upset with herself for losing control and not keeping the complete picture of her relationship with her daughter in mind.

To me, Sharon's experience and reactions are part of the educational process that goes on for the parent. Sharon needs to tell Heather that certain things on the computer just aren't acceptable for a ten-year-old. Heather is a normal child; her mom had found her just browsing, not particularly looking for sexually explicit material. She needs to be taught that this material isn't appropriate for her. Sharon is screaming, "How can you look at this?" or asking her, "What's wrong with you?" doesn't deal with the issue. Instead, this emotional outburst encourages Heather to defend what she's done. While it may be shocking for a parent to witness their child's exposure to graphic content, they must always remember to **stay calm**, and think before they respond. Rationally explaining to Heather the simple truth that there are some inappropriate sites on the Web is how to deal with the situation. Just as talking to strangers can be bad, so can being in the wrong places on the Web. This is a new generation with new problems.

In this age where electronic communications have so much power, parents need to be especially vigilant concerning their children. So Sharon and Heather's dad had a talk about the Internet, people who look for children on it, and the dangers of these kinds of activities. Saying "no" in this way makes it an invaluable learning process, not a punitive or harsh reaction to which the child will not listen and from which she will not learn. The child will not be defensive because he/she is not being attacked. This discussion brought mom, dad and Heather closer by making Heather feel that her parents understand the Web and her attraction to being on-line with her friends. Sharon felt good about handling this situation well, and her younger child will also benefit one day from what she learned.

Grade School — The Age to Teach Values, Limits and Goals

Because kids are bright and savvy about so many things, parents sometimes assume that kids will absorb values by osmosis the way they absorb information about TV shows and fashions. Many kids don't know as much as some parents think they do. By the time children reach age six or seven, they are more and more able to understand general ideas and values. However, parents can't expect them to learn the values they want them to learn from friends, television, or the Internet. Parents have to teach their kids the basic values they want them to absorb.

Sara, age six, has made plans to play with one friend after school, but she now wants to spend the afternoon with another friend, Melissa, because she is more "cool." Sara is struggling with trying to play with certain kids such as Melissa, the more popular kids in her circle, but her mom thinks there is a lesson in this situation. Of course she understands that her daughter wants to be popular and spend time with the cool kids, but she doesn't want to send Sara the message that it's okay to break play dates whenever she wants to be with the popular kids. By age six Sara should be able to start to understand about keeping social commitments.

So mom tells Sara that the answer is "no" to her request to play with Melissa, not because she wants to keep her from Melissa, but because she has promised to play with someone else. She explains to her that sometimes life is about hard decisions like this and that there is always a tomorrow to play with Melissa. In this case, mom had a difficult time because Sara is an insistent child, and with verbal skills to match those of an adult, she keeps up the pressure on her mother to have her way. So mom, who understands Sara and her temperament, came to my office, trying to deal with a child whose demanding, high-strung temperament is so different from her more passive, easygoing one.

Another high-strung child who was uncomfortable accepting boundaries and restraints, nine-year-old Brian, was trying to convince his parents that watching wrestling was okay just before bedtime. It seemed to me that Brian was already too wound up and wrestling just stimulated him more, making bedtime even more of a problem for him and his parents. They agreed with me that the request was not reasonable. They decided instead that Brian could stay up and do whatever he liked, but he could not watch wrestling. Of course Brian wasn't happy with this, but he understood that he wasn't able to sleep after watching wrestling. Mom and dad stayed focused and calm while they explained their decision (something they could not have done successfully with a toddler or a preschooler).

Some time after, I had this conversation with Brian and his parents.

Norma: *Brian, it sounds to me that you want to be the boss. Is that true?*

Brian: *Yes, I want to be the boss of the house, but my parents won't let me.*

Norma: *Do you know why you can't be boss? (This was said with much humor in the room.)*

Brian: *Why?*

***Norma:** Well, you have to be grown up and be working and making money before you can be a boss.*

***Brian:** Really!*

***Norma:** How about asking mom and dad if you can be boss of one thing this week?*

***Brian:** I would like to be the boss of my showers.*

***Norma** (to Brian's parents): Mom and dad, can Brian decide when he will take his showers this week? (Brian's mother had begun to control more and more as he got older. Brian and mom were at the point of arguing about everything, including shower time.)*

***Brian's Parents:** Yes.*

Notice what happened here. First, Brian was allowed to speak his feelings, and his parents had to listen. No one was screaming, even though they wanted to. There was humor in the room. Brian felt understood, and was given the autonomy (although not the power), to choose what he wanted to be the boss of. His request was reasonable, and his parents agreed to it. It was the first time there was a calm. Although the idea of the shower seems ridiculous, it was the beginning of a give-and-take situation.

At our next meeting, Brian told me that he and his mom had had a better week. His parents were working hard at saying "yes" to his reasonable requests, and when they said "no," there was no yelling. They displayed more humor; something they realized had been lost. They were a working team, and as they continued to work at it, Brian began to calm down. His outbursts became less frequent; he was becoming less angry. Recently he even complimented his mother on her ability not to yell at him when he was wrong. He told her that he was proud of her. Brian has progressed quite a lot. The visits to my office have been reduced.

Mom is letting go of some of her control. Dad is supporting mom on issues that were major problems. As mom feels more supported by dad, there has been a sense of teamwork in the home. Brian even told them that they needed to hug more.

Another important issue at this age is schoolwork. When David, who is seven, wants to play instead of reading his science book, dad has to emphasize to him the importance of school and what is expected of him. Dad discussed the importance of school and the idea that although playing may be more fun than reading, life brings responsibilities, and one of his is to do well in school. David and his dad talked about the value of setting goals and about how we reach them. David was able to express his feelings about the ideas his father presented and learned that despite them, rules had to be followed. Dad stuck to his point and kept calm. This was the beginning of discussions about goals as this is the age that values and responsibilities should be taught. Dad was planning to help his son set some simple goals and to watch to see if they had been realized. There was no yelling, no screaming but a good lesson for David.

Factoring in Feelings

Some situations involve deeper emotional feelings that need to be handled in special ways. For instance, Sam, age twelve, wanted his mother to sit with him because he couldn't concentrate on his homework when she wasn't around. On the surface, Sam's request might not seem reasonable, but to me it was because of his family history. Sam's dad died when Sam was seven, and even though he has a very high IQ, he had a hard time keeping his sadness at his father's loss from distracting him from studying. One week I asked him, “Sam, is there one subject that you can do on your own?” He said, “I think I could do my math but I have trouble with social studies.” I told him I understood and that I expected him to try his math on his own and do his social studies with mom. This was a reasonable request. Although Sam's mom wants him to learn to study independently, she has decided that being angry with him just isn't working and that sitting with him and getting him started is the better way. She also understood Sam's unresolved grief was affecting his concentration and that she needed to talk to him about his father's death. She discussed her feelings with me, as a way of learning more about Sam's needs at that moment. He would one day be able to be alone with all of his feelings, but just then they were too difficult, as the sadness of his father's death had not been dealt with adequately.

Usually, parenting problems are easier to uncover. Stephanie, for instance, age six, is an only child of parents who can, and do, give her everything. Stephanie's parents are in my office because they realize that their daughter wants to run the house. She is highly verbal, with the negotiating skills of a much older child and a temperament that finds it hard to "go with the flow." As a result of Stephanie's intelligence, verbal skills and her parents' inclinations to say "yes" to her because of their circumstances, there have been few "no's" in her life so far.

Stephanie's parents came to me because they were yelling at Stephanie and getting nowhere with her. They told me that they couldn't make her do anything that she didn't want to, and we agreed that this could be a problem. Stephanie is also overweight, and my guess is that her eating habits reflect her out-of-control behavior. Stephanie's parents realized that their daughter was angry at their yelling at her so much, but they were just as angry. When I asked Stephanie, "What are your parents going to do?" she had the wisdom to answer, "My parents will have to figure that out by themselves." Stephanie's parents were shocked at this answer, but it was the right one: They would have to develop a plan for dealing with Stephanie.

They have agreed with Stephanie that they will not yell at her, and they are working on replacing angry outbursts with more focused, directed responses. They have brought Stephanie to see me several times, and they will continue to do this as they acquire more skills in modeling appropriate behavior for Stephanie. They are committed to trying to stay calm. The other issue will be food, a difficult one because of the influence of television and peer pressures. I am hopeful that it can be brought up soon. If Stephanie doesn't want to talk about it, I'll have to wait until she is ready to do so.

I'm engaged in these kinds of discussions with kids and parents every day in my office. I help parents stay calm while they hear what their children feel. It's not easy for parents to hear their six-year-old child say about them, "They can't make me do anything." This is the first step toward getting their power back, no matter how long it takes. Stephanie's mother thanked me for helping her control her feelings, and I was sure that she and her husband would be working to find the right words and behaviors to feel strong in dealing with their overly empowered child. Stephanie also sensed that I was going to help the family. Like most of the children who see me, she realizes that I like kids and therefore she enjoys coming to my office.

Recently, Mark, who is twelve, was in my office for the first time. He had been acting out against his parents for some time, and his mother was about to punish him again for making a disrespectful gesture to his father in front of his (Mark's) friends. When Mark's dad lost his temper then and screamed at him, Mark reacted in the defensive way typical of someone of his age and denied what he had in fact done. This got Mark's dad even angrier with him. In telling his side of the story to me, Mark explained that even though he knew it was wrong to lie, he was trying to protect himself in front of his friends (it is very hard for a twelve-year-old to admit to anything less than perfection).

I realized why Mark's parents were upset, and I felt that Mark needed help in understanding that he couldn't treat his father so disrespectfully, especially not for the purpose of impressing his friends. After further discussion, I also realized why this incident had happened and how Mark's father could have handled things differently. We were all able to see that another issue, rivalry between Mark and his brother, was at the root of the flare-up. Mark had been upset about a quarrel with his brother, and his behavior toward his father may have been his way to call attention to his feelings. By jumping in and reacting angrily and accusingly, Mark's father had missed identifying the deeper issue.

Mark was amazingly well behaved and expressive for a twelve-year-old at his first time in a stranger's office and was able to say, "I tried to get any attention I could — negative, positive, or whatever." He had his mother's attention, and I made sure that she listened. Then Mark had to listen to his mother. I added a touch of humor, and by the time they left, mother and son were smiling at one another.

Although Mark's parents wanted to punish him, my feeling was that Mark was being punished so often that he was getting negative attention; their punishment was actually fueling his aggressive behavior. I felt that instead Mark needed to be with his mother and that she and his father needed to learn how to say "no" to Mark without making him feel he was a terrible child who could do no right. After I pointed these ideas out to Mark's parents, they were very open to them and took my lead. His mother brings Mark to my office every week and also takes care to spend special time with him. These interactions have been very helpful.

"Yes" Is Also Important to Grade Schoolers

I tell parents to be careful of saying too many "no's" to grade school kids and to say "yes" often enough so that when the "no's" come, as they must, they will be more tolerable. At this age, when children are now able to understand more general ideas and values, parents should teach them rather than yelling at them. When you are unhappy about some new demand or behavior of your child, you should address the values and issues that underlie your reaction. Try not to get too emotionally caught up in **attitudes** that may seem shocking or repulsive on the part of your child (this will come even more for teenagers). Instead, deal calmly and rationally with behavior that you are unhappy about. Restraining some of your natural and negative emotions and trying to understand your child's feelings may be difficult, but creating a bond with your children that will help you and them in the future will reward you.

Five Common Scenarios and Interventions for Saying "No" to Your Grade Schooler

• **Example 1**

Your grade schooler has just punched his younger sister in the stomach.

The dad wants to hit the child and scream, "What the hell is wrong with you!!??"

What you can say... "You are never to hit your sister, and we do not hit girls, ever!!" Your voice should rise here. Yelling is understandable and appropriate. Parents need to be strict with discipline. The child should know that there will not be a second incident of this sort.

• **Example 2**

Your grade schooler wants to buy a dress that makes her look years older.

What you really want to say... "That dress makes you look terrible!!"

What you can say... "This dress is not appropriate for you. Your friends may have one, but this is our decision. I am sorry you are upset, but that is the decision. When you are older, you can look that way."

• **Example 3**

Your grade schooler wants to wear makeup and is pouring it on (the makeup, that is).

Fathers usually say "That's disgusting!"

Mom and dad need to sit down with the child and talk about what is reasonable, and the appropriateness of a lot of makeup. Find one thing you can all agree on her wearing, be it a little lipstick/ gloss or a little eye makeup. Do not attack the girl. The media and peers are tough competition, but what she does is up to you in the end.

• **Example 4**

Your grade schooler throws a baseball bat at practice, and shows a quitter type attitude.

What you really want to say... Fathers: "You are acting like a loser!! We're going home; you can't play this game if you are going to be a cry baby."

What you can say... This is your opportunity to discuss morals and values with the child. Sportsmanship, team spirit and getting along with others are at issue here. Your child may never become a New York Yankee, but that is not the point. We all need to learn to get along. This lesson will last them a lifetime, literally. Grade school is the time you want to set your child's values, because that will also determine the friends they keep and are drawn to. You can tell the child that this behavior is unacceptable, and that if they cannot behave properly they are not wanted in this environment. The behavior is dangerous and will NOT be tolerated, ever! The child needs to know this.

• Example 5

Your grade schooler is on the Internet too long and/or watching too much TV, and having difficulty in school. You receive a call from the teacher.

What you really want to say… "Your grades better go up or you're grounded."

Before you say anything, you must take on some of the responsibility. Sometimes as parents we allow this to happen one way or another. Kids are kids and do what is easiest and most fun. You must apportion your child time and give him a schedule to follow. This is the time for setting limits. A few years later will be way too late. Instilling the importance of goals, work ethic, and self-esteem should be the focus. The child will not be kicked out of school because of a low test score, nor will it affect his entire life.

The Teenage Years: "Wannabe Adults"

The Teenage Years: "Wannabe Adults"

A Profile of the Teenager

It's always important for parents to keep in mind what's happening to their children developmentally at each stage, and this is especially true when dealing with teenagers. Parents can expect to be constantly struggling with them over independence and safety issues. This is normal, common, and part of the healthful development of a teenager, and it can't happen without a tug of war, angry words, and angry tempers. It's the process that ultimately leads to the teenager and the parents letting go.

Friends reign in this period. Teenagers worry about who their friends are and whether they will be accepted. They often are preoccupied with where they stand socially. Because of this need for peer approval and acceptance by the "in-crowd", teenagers are extremely sensitive about their appearance. Their self-image is powerfully influenced by how they think their peers see them and about how they feel they fit the desirable image of a teenager presented to them by the pervasive and powerful media.

This is also a time of mood swings: Teenagers want to run their lives, but they still cannot. They feel competent at times, but afraid and insecure at others. At one moment they recognize that they still need help; the next moment, they get angry when parents treat them as anything less than mature adults. They are searching for their identity and trying to assert independence from parents and their parents' set of values. Most teenagers have found their opinionated voices, and are always trying to make a point or get what they want.

At this turbulent, inconsistent stage, as teenagers run from one emotional extreme to another, forbearance and even humor are often the best strategies for a parent. Teenagers are much more vulnerable to a world of drugs, alcohol, sexuality, eating disorders and affluence than when we were growing up. With the added peer pressures that affect them, we must be prepared and able to say "no" at the right time and model behavior to help teenagers be strong so that they can also make the often-difficult decision to say "no." Parents often fall into two patterns of extreme reaction to their teenagers: Some get too involved in their children's lives; others don't get involved enough. Reacting to every inappropriate or offensive word, action, or attitude of a teenager is a recipe for disaster; sometimes a teenager just needs to blow off some steam. At the same time, a parent needs to realize that a teenager is still very much in need of guidance and needs to be told "no" to unreasonable requests. Parents need to remember that the teenage years are perhaps the most tumultuous of stages. They need to understand when to let go and how to say what they are feeling without being punitive or harsh. At the same time, teenagers can rationalize and justify anything their friends want them to do with them and tell the parent, "You just don't understand." When this happens, parents need to make clear, "We do understand, but that's not an invitation to walk all over us!"

After giving all through the years without expecting any appropriate behavior in return, parents naturally get resentful and often ask me about their kids, "How can they ask for everything?" To this I answer them, "How could they not?" considering that they've been indulged with everything that they have wanted without any serious plans about parenting or any thought about what the consequences of not having a plan might be. At this point in his or her development, trying to out-yell your teenager will get you nowhere. Telling teenagers they are terrible for asking doesn't accomplish anything, either. This reaction, and comments such as "I'm tired of your behavior," "How can you be so immature," "You're so ungrateful," or "You're so incredibly selfish" just don't work.

These comments attack the teenager's character and personality, instead of addressing specific behaviors. They are the direct result of parental frustration at a situation that has probably not been dealt with adequately and has developed over a long period of time.

Some Basic Strategies

In times of difficulty, it may seem hard for parents and teenagers to believe that they can find mutual respect and then build a friendship, but they can, if they follow these strategies:

- Always look to be in sync with your spouse on how to deal with an issue before you confront your child. This way, kids who know their parents are a team can't go from one parent to the other in search of the "yes" word. If you are a single parent, decide how you are going to deal with an issue. Talk with a friend, relative or someone you admire if you are unsure. Make a plan and stick to it.

- Based on this common understanding let your teenager know what is expected of him or her before problems, requests, or demands develop.

- Don't react with anger or other uncontrolled emotions, even if the issue is serious or difficult to accept. Don't scream; instead, stay calm and respond. When your teen loses his or her cool, don't lose yours.

- Be prepared to say "yes" to reasonable requests. Don't say "no" just to "make a point" or assert your authority over your child. When you have to say "no," be honest about it. Don't conjure up some excuse to avoid your child's anger.

- Stick to the issues. Criticize inappropriate behavior, not who your teenager is.

- If you decide that punishment is called for, model good judgment by making it fit the behavior.

- Don't hold grudges. Instead of holding onto anger at previous negative or offensive actions, move forward.

Before seeing how these strategies operate in some conflicts I've worked at resolving between parents and their teenagers, let me reemphasize two other all-important principles brought up before: consistency and restraint. Parents cannot go from telling their children to grow up and then turn around and treat them like children. Parents need to hold their ground on important issues involving money, safety, moderation, and accepting the emotional, financial and practical responsibilities that come with adulthood. Sometimes this is difficult because teenagers are a bundle of contradictions, insistent on getting what they want, and will react to a "no" in very negative and disturbing ways.

This is where restraint comes in. In times of anger, your child may say things to you that you find offensive or insulting. Don't take everything he/she says literally. When you have said "no" to a request or have disagreed with your teenager, you must realize that he/she is going to be unhappy. Don't get stuck in that one moment of time when your child is reacting with anger because a minute later he/she may very well want to talk to you calmly and rationally. Again, remember the up-and-down nature of the teenager. If you keep badgering your child about one particular unpleasant moment, you are ignoring the emotional swings of your teenager.

Let's say your child is asking for another pair of sneakers and there are already ten pairs in the closet. Don't be shocked at this demand and call him or her selfish for asking. Keep in mind the influence of peers and the media — perhaps their friends have even more sneakers in their closets.

You can still teach your teenagers the appropriate values you want them to learn — in this case moderation, common sense, and not automatically giving in to every wish. Your child won't be happy with you for the moment, but as you've seen by now, continually giving won't solve anything; it will only encourage the teenager to keep demanding more and more. This in turn will only make your child feel bad about his or her inappropriate behavior without changing it. No one wins. However, keep in mind, if these issues were dealt with earlier in their development, then the interchange between parents and teens would be much more cooperative at this stage. However, for the parent who has not issued enough "no's" to their growing child and now has a defiant, rebellious teenager, well, ... you can look for that in my next book!

Reacting and Communicating Calmly

So how are you going to say "no" to a teenager who doesn't want to hear the word? You need to teach your children about values and moderation in a way that they can understand. The delivery of the "no" has to be done without anger or harshness. Even if the teenager is screaming and you want to scream back, keep a lid on that reaction because it will lead to a screaming contest. Along with a host of scathing remarks too offensive to be listed here, expect to hear the following:

- "You just don't get it!"
- "I hate you!"
- "You're different than the other parents!"
- "Jenny's parents are cooler than you!"
- "I wish I didn't live here!"

By reacting this way, the teen is trying to get the parent to have an emotional outburst, and when this happens, you have lost the round and he/she has won — it's that simple. Every time you lose control and lose focus, the "no" becomes a war. No one has gotten his or her point across, and you and your teen are on the same level — each looking to see who can scream louder.

As a parent, you may be confident that you can win this war, but this kind of victory doesn't mean anything if you haven't communicated what you want your child to learn.

So instead of these responses ...	Try these ...
"You're just lazy."	"I'm upset with your work."
"How can you ask for more privileges?"	"I understand you'd like to stay out later."
"How could you do something so stupid?	"I'm disappointed in your judgment."
"How can you think you're going to get into a good school with those grades?"	"Let's talk about your work habits and goals for the future."

The "no" should also be a consistent, honest, and rational one. A "yes" on Thursday should not be a "no" on Monday. And certainly, by the time a child becomes a teenager, he/she deserves an honest explanation of why the answer to a request is "no." Two major reasons for saying "no" at this age are finances and concern for safety. The more parents can be calm, the more they can communicate the issues to their teenager and use the situation as a learning experience and not a no-win battle.

I can recall that one of my most interesting teenage cases involved a family where the conflict had gotten so intense that my outside help was needed. The teen, Debbie, was unable to speak to her parents except to yell at them, "You're such idiots!" or similar phrases to express her anger when another "no" was directed at her. Debbie's parents didn't know how to handle her and didn't agree about what they should do.

They were just too angry, confused and frustrated to think or react clearly. Had they been able to talk with one another and help each other through the anger and come up with a plan of responding, and not reacting in anger to Debbie earlier in her childhood, they could have learned how to deal with her and her anger as a teenager. Because they hadn't, they and their daughter were thoroughly frustrated and at odds when they walked into my office.

After many consultations to discuss Debbie's anger and her parents' reactions, peace was attained in their home. I found out that this was a wonderful family, successful in many areas of life, and with great intentions, but in need of a parenting plan. Because there had been none for so many years, setting up a plan that worked would take some time. Debbie's parents needed to understand that Debbie was an unusual child with a stubborn, determined disposition. Screaming at her or calling her names did not work — as it doesn't in most conflicts with teenagers. All parties concerned had to get over the urge to vent the rage when they reached my office. Debbie's parents finally tried to stay calm — no simple task after years of overreacting to their daughter's anger. This was a good start.

Then, after months of talking, Debbie visited my office for Thanksgiving. I asked her how mom and dad were. I knew the answer because her mom was staying in touch with me, but I wanted to hear Debbie express her feelings about her parents. How happy I was to hear her say, "We just get along so well; mom and dad are fun to be with." "That's so great," I said. "I remember when you couldn't stand to be in the same room or the same solar system at the same time." Then Debbie summarized what this family had learned: "I think we all worked on not being so angry, and now we all listen, even when we don't agree with one another." Could Debbie's parents have done this with their daughter without me? Yes — coming to my office could have been an option rather than a necessity if they had been able to find comfort in and support for each other and agree on a plan earlier. Remember the old adage: "If you fail to prepare, you prepare to fail."

Saying "No" While Respecting Your Teenager's Feelings

Consider how two parents I've been counseling have dealt with their daughter Allie, who wanted to go with her friends to a party. She was fourteen and strikingly attractive, and her parents worried about her and the parties she had been asked to attend. They knew the parents at the home of Allie's next party, and they asked her if they were going to be home. They weren't satisfied with her answer, "I'm not sure, but it doesn't matter because Pam's brother, who's eighteen, will be there." Allie by then knew how to argue her point, and she was set on going. Her parents, though, had decided that she would not be allowed to attend any unsupervised parties. This was part of a plan, and they agreed to stand together and handle this together no matter how angry Allie got, so they were prepared for what might happen.

Allie raised her expected argument, and her parents just stayed focused on the issue of safety. For the first time, mom felt totally supported by dad. The "no" was well planned. It didn't attack Allie's judgment, and it showed her parents' understanding of her constant need for approval and acceptance by her peers. Allie responded with a tantrum, screaming, insults, and curses, but she knew that her parents weren't going to be swayed in their decision. As they had agreed beforehand, they continued to stay calm and didn't respond to Allie's outbursts. This took great strength and support from one another, but Allie's parents were determined to stand their ground, and that was the key.

Part of the conversation went like this:

***Allie**: Mom, Pam is having a party Saturday night, and everyone is going.*

***Mom**: Are her parents going to be home?*

***Allie**: I'm not sure, but Jonathan will be home. You know he's her older brother who is going to college soon. (This rationalization seems like logic to Allie, but in this case, it doesn't fool her parents.)*

***Mom:** Allie, you know dad and I have decided that we're just not comfortable with you being at parties without parents being home. We just feel better when we know parents are home.*

***Allie** (getting into a yelling mode}: But everyone will be there! I'll be the only one not allowed to go!*

***Mom**: Look, Allie, you know that your dad and I want you to have fun and be part of the group, but this is an issue of safety. We feel you and your friends are all too young to go unsupervised, especially after some of the problems at other parties. (Mom and dad remain calm.)*

***Allie** (storming out of the room): I hate you both!*

The tension in the room is high, and mom and dad have to deal with Allie's anger. Mom doesn't like having her daughter angry with her. She wants to rush into Allie's room and apologize, but she lets Allie have her feelings and stays close to her husband for support. Allie comes back a little later and makes small talk. No one brings up the tantrum — a major defense tactic with teens.

Allie is waiting to be yelled at, but this never comes. Everyone feels a sense of relief.

Allie's parents have taken a first step in regaining control of their teenager. They have said "no" to an issue of concern for them and one that will probably not be resolved quickly. Allie is fourteen, so there will be many parties, many "yes" words, and many "no" words in the future. Allie's parents realize that the world is not going to end when their teen is angry with them or when they are angry at their teen. They can respect their child's feelings without granting her every wish.

Learning to Listen More

One of my most challenging cases involved an exceptionally intelligent teenager, Jay, who is now seventeen and who first came to my office when he was fourteen because of his out-of-control behavior. His intelligence makes him one of those children who are not only academically brilliant, but analytically brilliant as well. Despite Jay's giftedness, his parents were afraid that he would not reach his potential, due to his impulsivity and poor judgment. His mother catered to him as a young child — now she is angry with him because he has no sense of who he is or of what responsibilities life requires. He just wants everything his way.

The level of arguing was so great that it ultimately led Jay's parents to my office. When they first walked in, I could see that they were a lovely family with an exceptional child who spoke like an adult. Jay's problem of being out of control was a family issue, with everyone screaming at one another and no one able to stop the cycle of destructive behavior. Jay's parents were so afraid of his potential for failure that they kept trying to push him, and the more they pushed, the more he defied them.

Jay and his parents spent a few hours in my office, with Jay spending the most time, talking about his family, his parents' criticism of him, and his need to be himself. He wanted to pick his own friends, but his parents objected that they were not on the same intellectual level as he was. He wanted to do his work when he wanted, not when his parents wanted him to. The negotiations were exhausting. I tried to keep each family member from making demands that were too extreme. At times the level of anger seemed unbearable to Jay, but he always called when he needed someone to listen to him. At times when he was wrong, I told him so, and at other times when I felt his requests were reasonable, I helped his parents see the wisdom of giving him more privileges. The calls from the family came in early in the morning or late at night. Whenever there was trouble, I got a call.

Finally, one morning came a breakthrough moment that changed Jay's relationship with his parents. After years of negotiating and arguing, Jay said to his mother, "Do you realize that you comment on everything I do from brushing my teeth to my homework? I can't do anything right. You scrutinize everything I do, and you aren't even aware of it." Happily, Jay's mom was able to hear his words at this point and accept them. Somehow, the timing of Jay's comments came at a time when his mother was ready to hear them. She had been working on the fact that Jay was so busy defying her that she was losing him. I told her she was more interested in winning battles than in winning the more important effort of getting Jay to trust and listen to her. Things finally seemed to make sense for her.

The next morning Jay's mother called to say she felt bad that Jay was so upset with her. A long talk followed; I told her that Jay was right — she and her husband never left Jay alone. They hadn't accepted him for who he is without a critical comment. I wasn't going to take away Jay's mom's feelings at that point; she needed to accept the fact that she felt bad and look at her behavior. She and her husband would be in my office tomorrow to discuss how to proceed with Jay — when to say "no," when to say "yes," and how to take who Jay is into consideration before they act. Even if they were worried, they probably needed to just let Jay be a teenager.

I know that Jay is a great kid with unusual talents, but I also know he is a teenager who sometimes acts like an adult and then switches to being seventeen. His parents needed to start with a new plan. As I write this chapter, Jay again has pushed the limit and just got in trouble for not using good judgment with a friend of his. His mother, though, handled the situation more calmly this time. Once again, there she discussed friendships with Jay and the importance of picking friends who have good character. Will Jay ever learn this lesson? I hope so, but in the meantime, his parents and I are not going to give up on him.

Teenagers need to feel some independence; they need to make mistakes and they need their parents to understand this turbulent period of their life. Parents have natural fears about their children going astray, but if they have taught their child well in his or her early years, they should recognize that being a teenager and slipping at times is normal and has to be expected. A low grade here and there doesn't mean your child will become a dropout, derelict or serial killer. All kids, including a unique child such as Jay, need to experiment at times. With all his brilliance and scholarships and awards, Jay is still a typical teenager who needs to find his way. A child who is exceptional will still mess up at times, but he/she can still be trusted to do the right thing more often than not. Parents need to know that debates and lashing out in anger are how teenagers move to a new stage in their life. Without this kind of conflict, a child may not be taking the important and necessary step of moving away from the family, which is really what the teenage years are leading to.

Disciplining Without Grudges

If your teenager has done something wrong, tell him or her and deal with the issue quickly. Don't hold grudges, and don't give too much attention to unacceptable behavior. For example, Leslie, one of the parents I'm working with, came in recently, absolutely brokenhearted that her fifteen-year-old Amanda had stolen a purse and the money in it from a baby-sitting job. To Leslie, this was about the most despicable act anyone could perform, and her level of rage and disappointment was high. Gordon, Amanda's dad, took Amanda's action as an expression of some deeper emotional conflict while Leslie reacted with a more personal sense of hurt. We talked with Amanda about a plan for returning everything she had taken and what the consequences for her actions would be. The most interesting part of this story, which did not surprise me because I knew how responsible Amanda was as a baby-sitter, was that the people she had taken the purse from wanted her back to continue baby-sitting for them.

We decided on a month of no outside activities except community service and religious attendance for Amanda, but this plan was changed because she was needed to help baby-sit during a family illness. Instead, all monies from Amanda's baby-sitting had to be given to her dad, and she would be watched more closely. Her summer plans were also dependent on good behavior.

We all knew that her taking the money was a way of getting attention, but as upsetting as Amanda's action was, I didn't want her to get constant attention for it. I wanted the consequences of the situation, including Amanda's need to be watched, addressed in my office. I knew that Amanda's younger sister, who was just coming into her teen years, had been given a great deal of attention for losing weight and that Amanda was involved in some major sibling-rivalry issues. It was time to talk about them in my office.

That was the plan we all agreed on. In doing so, Amanda's parents were in total agreement for the first time. I told Leslie that she should not treat Amanda like a criminal; that could make her turn into one. If we didn't dwell on this incident, I suggested, it would be one isolated moment in time. Amanda wasn't happy that her parents were so upset. When I asked her what she thought their reaction should be, she said, "They punished me, and now I'm trying to get their trust back. It should be over." That's how a teenager feels — "I did something stupid, but please don't punish me forever and treat me like a bad person."

The important thing was that Amanda's parents were now communicating. Their different styles had contributed to the problem; Leslie was very giving, but her husband never agreed with her. The emotional highs and lows of the week had brought the family together, and they were making a new beginning.

Being Prepared for Your Teenager

I'm not trying to minimize the challenges of raising teenagers. Most push their parents to the limit, and parents are naturally afraid of what could happen when they go beyond it. So many things can go wrong, so it's understandable that parents aren't always ready to handle problems that arise. These problems are especially difficult when they are one step from requiring more serious help. At times I've sensed serious issues (eating issues, for instance) that require a medical team. At times a psychiatrist has had to be consulted before any work could be done with a teenager — or other child, for that matter. Parents expect me to be truthful, and whatever the case, I tell them honestly if they need to consult with a doctor.

An angry teen is a concern for the entire family. Parents need to always be committed to working on teenage issues and not giving up or avoiding them. A child who is doing poorly in school or does not have friends or who seems unhappy needs parental help.

A child who is behaving appropriately for a teenager may not need so much attention, but he/she still needs the parent to be observant at this very secretive stage of life. Children can hide many problems just by spending their time on the Internet or on the phone. We should never think everything is okay just because kids seem happy in their room and aren't bothering us. We do not want to be the last to learn about a problem.

That's why the tragic shooting incident in Columbine is so horrifying and strikes at our deepest fears and emotions. Most of us, when we look at the teenage boys who did the shooting, wouldn't compare them to our children. Their parents clearly weren't on top of whatever their children were involved in. They had no idea that they were planning such a devastating act, much less harboring such murderous and disturbed thoughts. Being disengaged from a child's thoughts and feelings, however, is one step on the road to what happened at Columbine.

I tell parents to stay involved, to know whom their children are with, or even to check in each day with them to see how their lives are going. Ignorance or being busy is no excuse.

If the teenager's or parent's anger is too great, it comes from an earlier period, or involves some issue that the parent has not dealt with in his or her childhood, then parents may need to seek some other help. If the conflict is just a matter of everyday issues such as schoolwork, curfews, parties, friends, or spending and shopping, then parents and kids should be able to resolve it among themselves. If you are a single parent, you can often sort things out by yourself or with a friend. The most important point is being honest with your feelings. Teen issues can be taxing on parents, but if they are handled well — which to me means in a way that shows respect for the teenager and his or her development — then life with your teenager can be enjoyable, and your teenager can be fun to hang out with as he/she moves toward adulthood. Don't expect a "Thank you" when you say "no" to your teenager, but you may get one years later.

Often parents ask me of their teenagers, “How can I let them know that I care or that I am worried?” I tell them to voice their concerns honestly and openly, to discuss their kids’ options and think of solutions with them when they have a problem, and not to try to solve problems quickly without their kids’ input. Listen before you tell them what to do. Remember, times are different. Put yourself in your children’s shoes and take into account the fast-moving, media-dominated environment they are confronted with today.

If you still don’t know what to say, you can say that you want to think about the problem or discuss it with someone before you get back to him or her. Teenagers need guidance and they need to be heard. Telling them they are wrong for having a feeling is the most unhelpful comment that a parent can make at any age, but it is absolutely enraging and devastating to a teenager.

Stick with issues. Stay focused. Be honest. Listen. Be a prepared parent; it will ensure your success.

Dealing With Your Defiant Teen

Perhaps the most upsetting and the greatest challenge to a parent comes when a child grows into a defiant teenager. At this point, partly because of the child’s stage of development, saying “no” is much less effective. Adolescents want independence; they want to run their own lives and make their own rules. Parents will encounter common acts of defiance such as breaking curfews, lying, sneaking a drink, or taking the car without permission. In these kinds of situations, you can express your disappointment and anger, reprimand, punish, ground, or take away privileges from your child. If your child appears to you as the one in control, you still have influence and control over him or her. Your child is simply a normally defiant teenager who seeks independence and/ or attention but who still respects you and needs your acceptance.

If children never hear the word "no," they will reach a higher level of defiance until a parent can no longer control them. At this level, she may be afraid not only for her child, but also of her child. The child may have a drug and/or alcohol problem, an eating disorder, or a psychological disorder or he/she may be a member of a gang. The child may be so alienated or so defiant at this point that nothing a parent can say has any impact. At this point it is probably necessary to consult a professional for help. Failure to do so may result in a parent's worst fears coming true.

More Examples...

If your child is a teenager, and you have found it hard to say "no" to him or her, there is still time to assert yourself. Let's look at some more examples of common conflicts between parents and their teenage children.

Andrew is a fifteen-year-old on the verge of getting his driver's license. He is strong willed, opinionated and sassy-mouthed. His grades in school have slipped to C's, and now he wants to drive as do all his friends. Because Andrew used to be an A student, his mom and stepfather are not too pleased with his recent academic performance and certainly don't want to reward him with a car and license. So his mom, Barbara, has got a serious problem, especially as Andrew is now at a point in his life when he loves to fight with her at any time and place. She is torn with guilt about saying "no" to Andrew. One the one hand, she doesn't want to deprive him of what he wants or to make him feel left out. She doesn't want to feel like a bad mom or for Andrew to be angry, however, she is furious with her son's attitude of entitlement about having a car.

So does Barbara tolerate these unpleasant feelings and do what she knows she should, or does she give in to avoid World War III with Andrew? After thinking about things and discussing the matter with her husband, Barbara trusts her judgment and lays down these ground rules to Andrew: "Your grades come first. If you improve your grades you can get your license and you will be allowed to drive."

Andrew did not like this response to his demands, but Barbara stayed calm, and focused, and Andrew got the point. They both worked through a period during which they owned their anger and frustration with each other. He knew who was boss, and he understood that he wouldn't get his license unless his grades improved. Within a month, Andrew's grades improved. Barbara had taken control of the situation, set limits and said "no" despite whatever unpleasant feelings she had.

Here is another example: Nikki is seventeen. Last month she went to a party at her best friend, Robin's, house while Robin's parents were away. When Nikki came home at 11:30p.m., her curfew time, her mom and dad were up watching a movie and began talking to her.

They noticed she "wasn't all there" and that her breath smelled of alcohol. She admitted that she had had a drink. Her parents told her that she was underage and was not allowed to drink. They expressed their disappointment and talked to her about the dangers of alcohol abuse. Rather than yelling at or punishing Nikki, her parents kept their heads, realizing that a certain amount of rebelliousness and testing of limits is part of being a teenager.

Then, three weeks later, Robin's parents were away again and Nikki wanted to stay overnight at Robin's house. We all know what would be going on at Robin's house. So as Robin's parents, what do you do to prevent her from drinking? Do you tell her "no," totally devastate and infuriate he, and confront the "I hate you;" "Everyone else will be there" scenario? Or, to avoid feeling like a bad parent, do you let her go where you know she will be up to no good and where her safety is at risk?

You don't have to act impulsively, you can take your time thinking about how to handle the situation and discuss it with your spouse or with other parents. However, the correct decision, from my experience as a parent and as a family consultant, is clear: you must focus on the issue of your child's safety and say "no." Understanding that your child is going to be angry, you should not allow her to manipulate you into doing something you know is wrong.

It is our job to say "no" in these situations. If parents could do this more often and weren't so afraid of their children's feelings, rage and the uncomfortable feelings they invoke in us, we would be in control of them. Our children would not be so empowered and would not come to us with the "Everyone else's parents are letting them" excuse for giving into their demands.

Five Common Scenarios and Interventions for Saying "No" to Your Teenager

- **Example 1**

Your teenager stays out late and does not call, and you do not know his whereabouts. He shows up early the next morning.

What you really want to say... "Where the hell have you been? We've been up all night. What are you, a moron?" Many parents would want to strike the child. Another line is "You are so ungrateful! You never even think of us after everything we've given you!!"

What you can say... Although it may be tough, you need to remain calm. Tell the child sternly that the behavior is unacceptable and thoughtless. Tell the child "I know you are embarrassed to call in, but it has to be done. If your friends belittle you it is tough luck. You will not engage in unsafe activities as long as you live under our roof."

• Example 2

Your teenager is smoking... You found a pack of cigarettes in her pocketbook.

What you really want to say..., "Are you crazy? This can kill you!!"

What you can say... If the child has asthma be very stern and say "What you are doing can kill you! There is no way I am going to condone this behavior! If you persist you may damage your body permanently." Explain the risks and related problems that smoking causes. Use this opportunity to discuss drugs and alcohol.

• Example 3

Your teenager is thirteen and feels fat and says so.

What you really want to say... if the child IS fat: "No, you're not fat, you're beautiful!"

What you can say... If the child is fat or not, ask them, "What gives you that feeling?" This will open the dialogue and lead to many issues. If the child is fat, ask her if she wants some help in losing weight. If the child is not fat continue the dialogue and ask the child what she wishes to have. Ask her about her friends, and what brought it up in her mind. Tell her that you are proud, and give the child hope. Hope is what all children really NEED. If you exercise regularly and watch what you eat, you CAN be a great model for them to follow. If you are out of shape, and these issues apply to you as well, you really need to look inward, and ask yourself what can you do to help yourself. Then you can truly help your child.

• **Example 4**

Your teenager seems to want everything, and there is no limit to what they ask for.

What you really want to say… It really doesn't matter, you know what you want to say, and money actually does grow on trees!

What you can say… "Look, I know you think we are millionaires, but we are not. You can't always have everything you want, and there are limits in everything in life. Every family is different, and although some of your friends may have more, lots of people have less." They survive and so will you. Your teenager will not be happy and will probably storm out of the room as well. NO ONE likes to hear the word "no". This discussion should probably have taken place about ten years earlier.

• **Example 5**

Your teenager is drinking and comes home drunk with the car. He has also just gotten his driver's license.

What you really want to say… You are beside yourself. There are no words to sum up what you are feeling.

What you can say… "You have just endangered your life and the lives of countless others. This behavior is not only unacceptable, but stupid and reckless as well. You not only could go to jail for DUI or DWI, but you could end up with a charge of vehicular manslaughter. You are grounded indefinitely and you will be going to counseling. There are no options here for you and the matter is not up for negotiation. You had better sober up!!" This is not the time to be meek. You need to be harsh. Keys and license go out the door at this point. Go with your gut on this one.

Conclusion

How many times have we as parents felt that our child wants everything he/she sees and expects to get everything he/she asks for?

How does a child get to this point? It's a gradual process. The parent starts by giving the child everything they ask for, and before the parent realizes it, the child just expects more and more. They child also expects the parent to do everything, from putting toys away, cleaning up, getting dressed and doing homework. The child doesn't hear the word "no" and just assumes that he/she will just continue to be catered to. Then the parent gets mad at the child for being so demanding and acting as if they are entitled to everything.

At this point the parent wants to regain control, but the child does not want to give it up. This is usually the time when the parents come to me for help.

I work with parents to regain control of their families. I also work with the children in order to help the entire family unit function better. We start slowly and we develop a plan. The plan involves responsibilities for the parents and the children.

I encourage parents to model appropriate behavior, communicate and understand the importance of everyone's feelings. I help them to establish goals and boundaries, set realistic expectations and to understand their children's requests and behaviors. I help parents say "no" when they need to and to realize that they will still love you. Thus, they are empowered and can regain control of their families. I also help by giving children some responsibility, even if it's as small as picking the dishes up off the table.

Parents may start to give children certain chores to do so they can feel that there are expectations of them. I encourage them to explain expectations and goals to children from an early age so they can learn how a family functions, and prepare for working in their adult life. Children should be made part of a team in the home. If they are starting school, a key role of parenting is to explain what is expected of them there, such as listening to teachers and doing homework.

I hope this book has convinced you that your children will love you when they respect you and see that you have their welfare in mind. They may not like you when you say "no" to them, but liking or disliking a parent for a fleeting moment is not the issue. The real issue is what kind of children you want to raise in the long term. Children who are given too much don't feel that they have to work hard for things. Children who are rewarded or indulged for unacceptable behavior feel they can do whatever they want without any consequences. This kind of parenting clearly won't prepare a child for taking responsibility and living in a world with rules when he/she reaches adulthood. Children need limits so they can grow and prosper.

If we look beyond the concerns of our immediate families, the issue I'm raising looms even larger. What kind of adults do we want our children to become?

In the twenty-first century, with more technology, more affluence, more competition, and more demands on everyone, the pressures and challenges of parenting are greater than ever. To meet them, we have to be mindful of the world our children live in and teach them right from wrong at an early age. The centerpiece of this book is having a plan in order to teach our children values, morals, and most important, how to live responsibly.

My message is simple, and this is its essence:

- Communicate with your children.
- Listen to them.
- Model appropriate behavior for them.
- Understand the importance of feelings, theirs and yours.
- Learn when and how to say “no” to them.
- Say “yes” to their reasonable requests.

Using these strategies will enable you to raise strong, responsible, emotionally healthy, loving children and families.

The Most Commonly Asked Questions In My Office

Why is it so difficult for parents to ask for help with parenting?

You might wonder why in a time when so many of us are so educated and so successful at our work — why is it so hard to ask for help? Do we think because we are so successful in other areas, that it should be automatic and we should know how to be effective parents? Is it a personal blow to our egos when we have to reach out and ask for help? Whom do we go to for help? Do we have to go back to therapy and admit we are having a problem? Why do we wait until the school has called and said, "Your child is having a problem," before we look closely at what is going on?

Not everyone needs professional help in dealing with the day-to-day problems of raising healthy, well-adjusted children. Sometimes, when things are beyond our control, we need to turn to others for solutions. Parents should look to find help without feeling as if they are failing as parents. My experience has been that parents have a great deal of difficulty making that initial phone call, yet after they spend an hour in my office they relax because they have taken the first step and they usually feel that they are not alone. It is common for me to hear that they have been thinking of making the call but they usually feel that they will be able to solve the problem.

When the school calls, time's up! They are forced to look at the problem quickly or the child will then be forced to talk to someone at the school. Often, parents want this handled on the outside. Even if the child is seeing a professional the parent realizes that they must address the problem.

Often, the problem has to do with setting limits or boundaries. Other times, the child is not focused in his work. Aggressive behavior is another warning sign. The parent then needs to understand what is happening in the child's life. This is the reason that I am a firm believer in the process of communication from the beginning of the child's life, so that the child comes to the parent when they are experiencing any difficulties. So the road leads back to the idea of the lines of communication, which need to be open from the beginning.

Parents should not be afraid to get help and I hope that this book will help them consider the idea of reaching out for help as a positive move, not as proof that they are not being effective as a parent.

I think that parents have the notion that they should automatically know everything when it comes to parenting. Unfortunately, we live in a world where parents are always questioning their skills. We wonder if we are depriving our children, overindulging them, being fair or even if we are being too much of a friend as opposed to their role as a parent.

Yes, it can be overwhelming, and there is much to be afraid of when we are raising our kids. Will they be on drugs? Will they have an eating disorder? Will they be happy? Yes, it is an awesome responsibility to raise children in an age where so much can go wrong and when the peer group is so important.

I think the answer is to remember that we need to look at parenting early on and adopt a philosophy, which will make the road less difficult. If we are not afraid to look for help and feel that it is okay not to know everything, then there is hope that we will always be looking to improve.

What is the role of the father in the parenting process?

We always think of the mother as the nurturer, so what exactly does the father do? What is his role in making the family run smoothly?

Although many men will not like this answer, my feeling has always been that the father should support the mother so that she is able to run the family in a more cooperative manner. This really means that if a mother feels supported by the father, she feels stronger as a mother, and she feels better in her role as mother and wife. If the mother is the one who is home more, or who assumes more of the responsibility for the day-to-day care of the children, it is important that her emotions do not get in the way of her parenting.

After studying families for more than twenty years, it is clear to me that women who feel that the father is helpful and supports them with the children are happier, and thus more effective in their parenting role (not to mention it makes for a strong marriage).

A mother is asking her child for some help. The father says to the child, "Your mother needs some help. Please give her a hand." This type of comment can help the child learn that mom and dad are a team; to a child this is a great message. To the mother it is a message of support and the mother is then happy with the father. It is a positive situation for the entire family.

Often simple comments of support go a long way to promote a feeling of cooperation in the family. My feeling has always been that modeling behavior for our children helps them to learn. Telling them what to do, if it is not being done in the family, does not work as well as modeling. This parental support also goes the other way. When the father wants the child to do something, the mother can in turn support him. Any parental disagreements should be handled without the children's hearing them.

Fighting in front of the kids just makes them upset. With all the talk of divorce, it can give them ideas that may be completely unfounded. Parents should be able to present a united front for their children, even if they are not in total agreement. Children like to see their parents getting along. It makes them feel more secure.

When parents decide to work on their issues away from the children's listening range the atmosphere in the home improves. Parents who are cooperative with one another are helping their children to become more cooperative. Modeling positive, cooperative interaction for our children is the best way to help them grow up to be responsible and cooperative with others. It will help them fit into a world that requires a great deal of cooperation in order to be successful. Children must learn these basics for school, work and their future relationships.

What can I do when I see a problem and my child is not communicating? When should I seek outside help?

I want parents to think that there is hope when they see a problem. Although I want to urge parents to work on a plan of early involvement, so that there a fewer problems, I want them to know that there are always issues that come up as they parent. If the issues are addressed in a timely fashion, life is much simpler. Often, parents feel that the child will outgrow a certain behavior as they mature. That could happen. If the parent can think about the issues in a positive way and look at the idea of communication as a basic, then any issue can be discussed and worked through. This eliminates the parent's constant concern — have I done everything that I could? Every day that I sit with parents convinces me that they want to do their job well. They are concerned parents who want the best for their children. They seek information about parenting just as they would seek information on other topics.

The ones who end up in my office with younger children have different problems than the ones with older children. I would hope that when a parent identifies a problem and does not know what to do that they turn to someone they trust such as another parent or their doctor to get the name of someone who understands the field of parenting and who can guide them through the problem.

Getting a new focus does not mean that parents are inadequate in their roles. If your child is not communicating, then there must be some creative input to change how the family is functioning. Children need their parents, and parents need to know what their children are feeling. If they can figure the problem out by themselves, then that is wonderful. If not, then the parent must seek some help even if the child is resistant to the idea.

Children often have countless excuses for not wanting help (this is called resistance). Parents should understand that they are in charge and they must figure out the plan. Children cannot be in charge of these problems. That is the reason a parent must take charge and be the parent the child needs. The parent must never give up, even if the child is very resistant. Resistance is normal and must be dealt with.

The parent then needs to seek help first without the child. Sometimes the parent can turn things around without the child. New ideas for communication are discussed with a professional and the child benefits without going for help. Other times, parents find ways of eventually getting their children to go with them. Every family is different and needs a different solution. People need to be creative when there is a problem. They also need to be clear about the fact that they are not going to give up until the problem is solved.

Children whose parents are committed to not giving up are more hopeful because they know they do not have the tools to change the course that they are following. If they feel their parents are weak, then they know they are in serious trouble.

How do I get my child to talk to me?

This is a question that parents often ask when they see their child in their room or on the phone with friends. A parent may feel the child is avoiding them and that can be true. Often times, teenagers enjoy their friends' company more than their parents. The issue that's important is really quite simple: Is the child behaving in an age-appropriate manner and just being a normal kid, or is there a problem?

Does the child feel that the parent does not understand them and that their friends are better listeners? If that is the case, then the parent needs to figure out what they are doing to push their child away. Sometimes, parents are on a different track and do not understand what their child is feeling. If that is the case, then it is important to find out what has happened and figure out what to do about the situation.

I tell parents that they need to set up the lines of communication early on in the child's development rather than later on when there is a problem. It is very simple to ask small children how they are, what they are feeling and find out what they are thinking. The questions can be as simple as finding out what happened at school or with a friend.

The parent needs to listen when the child may feel upset with them. Telling a child that you understand their feelings or their hurt makes them feel understood. Children who feel their parents are listening will want to talk to them when times are good and, most of all, when they have a problem.

It is a wonderful gift to give a child — the feeling that his/her parents are listening and they love him/her. Later on, as they grow, it will be difficult to listen to some of their thoughts because of what they may be experiencing, but the idea is to let them know that even if you do not agree with them, you understand what they are feeling.

If your children are still young now, then you can apply some of these solutions right away. If your child is older and does not want to talk, find out what has happened. Ask the child what you can do about the problem. Tell them you would like to understand what has happened and that you are eager to remedy the situation. If they tell you that you are not listening — accept their perception and tell them you are planning to work on the problem.

Ask them for help and listen to what they say. Accept responsibility that you as the parent may be less than perfect, but that you are always trying to improve.

How do I know if my child has a learning problem?

Often parents think that a child is not doing his or her work because they simply don't want to do it. However, sometimes a child who seems to be having a problem concentrating, or who is constantly distracted or fidgety, may be having a problem that needs addressing in a more formal manner. They may need educational testing, remedial help or even some counseling. The parent must find the right learning specialist to get a proper evaluation.

Your child's school staff will often be the one to point out a potential learning disability. However, if they don't identify the potential problem for you, it may be necessary to request special testing for your child.

Perhaps the child cannot see the blackboard or has difficulty hearing. Perhaps the child has a hard time sitting still long enough to focus. These are all issues for a specialist. After some testing is done, the evaluator will have some recommendations. Sometimes the parent will learn that the child is suffering from Attention Deficit Disorder (ADD), or some other type of learning disability. The important focus here is to find the right team to work with your child. When the parent has consulted with the team of specialists, be they psychologists, learning specialists, or psychiatrists, the child will feel that they are being helped.

Children who feel hopeless about their problems are naturally less able to do their work or concentrate. When parents consult with me for their children, I use a team or specialists who determine the treatment plan. They all work together with the parent to help the child. The school is consulted and they become part of the solution as well.

Often, if the parent is in need of help, they may ask their pediatrician to make a referral to the right person. Parents usually find out early in a child's development that there may be a problem. Sometimes, parents feel the child will grow out of the problem or the child will mature and be able to concentrate when they are older. Sometimes, this is true, but often problems do not go away, and even get bigger if left untreated. Parents who address the problems early on in a child's life are much better able to help find solutions before the problem gets out of hand. Left untreated, learning difficulties can create self-esteem problems for the child because they cannot keep up with their classmates.

Early intervention or evaluation is good for everyone. Children feel relieved when the parents understand the problem. Parents feel happy when their child turns the corner and begins to learn and succeed in school. The child with a good level of self-esteem is more likely to perform better in school.

How do we handle children when there has been a divorce?

The topics of divorce, separation and blended families are a part of our world. Our children meet other children and often get acquainted with divorce either within their own family or as a part of someone else's family. One hears about divorce on a daily basis. A child whose family becomes part of a large statistic does not have to feel alone. There are support groups in school for children as well as constant conversation with other friends. Kids are experiencing the consequences of broken families at a rate that is quite alarming.

Can children be healthy even when they are the children of divorced parents? Sure they can. Children can grow up knowing that both parents care about them — that the children are not responsible for the breakup and that they have two parents who are interested in their welfare even if they are not living together. Some children end up with stepparents that adore them and therefore have even more people that care about them.

This is the ideal situation. However some children are not so lucky — parents are always feuding and cannot put their own needs aside. They cannot stop the endless bickering and then the children are put in the difficult and unfair position of trying to decide whom to be loyal to and whom to be angry with.

It is an unfortunate situation that too many children are exposed to without any choice or power. They are helpless pawns in a situation that they did not create. I hope that the parents will be smart enough to get professional help for these children so that they can succeed in life and school in spite of the pressures they are under.

There are many children who come into my office who have had parents who argue, yet have had loving stepparents who provide as much love as they need. There are also children who come to my office who are torn between two parents but at least they have help to deal with the many feelings that they are experiencing.

My advice to parents is to provide their children with as much outside help as possible if they see that the divorce is causing too much pain. Parents must be sensitive to their child's feelings as they go from house to house as part of the breakup. Let children discuss the pain with you. If you cannot tolerate the child's feelings, then a counselor will be able to provide some comfort.

Children often feel torn and prefer talking to someone other than their parent. Whatever the situation, listen to your child and look to others for the solutions if you are unable to find them yourself.

Divorce is a fact of life in today's world. That doesn't mean that children who feel that they are being treated well and who feel loved don't have every chance to be as healthy as possible in difficult times.

The focus is to help children express their thoughts, while respecting their feelings as one would in an intact family. Children of divorced parents will naturally have fears about the separation and what people will say and how they will handle the new people who come into their parents' lives. They may feel jealous, hurt or abandoned. A sensitive parent will understand that these are all normal feelings that are okay to express. If a parent tries to tell the child they should not have these feelings, then the child may start to repress these thoughts and other problems will then likely occur.

Once again, parents must understand that children of divorced parents will have many feelings that they may not like, but that they must accept. These feelings are normal and even healthy during their parents' breakup. Parents can use this time to reassure their children that they still love them, and will be there for them to help them get through the bad feelings and difficult times, no matter what. As always, communication, honesty and listening to your children's fears and concerns is paramount in importance.

How do you teach a child to be kind to others and to respect other children's feelings and thoughts?

Parents often ask about what to tell their children when they are behaving in a manner that is inappropriate. Sometimes parents allow their children to do or say things that are hurtful to other children. The parent may excuse the behavior with a remark such as, "Oh, they are just playing," or, "Boys will be boys." Instead, it is imperative that we stop a particular behavior and tell the child in clear terms that we do not make fun of other children.

Parents need to take charge of these types of situations because not saying anything gives the child the feeling that what they are doing is acceptable when it may not be. When parents see their child doing something that might be hurtful to another child, a parent needs to let their child know, in a sensitive way, that their behavior is unacceptable. As parents, our children look to us for direction on what is right and wrong. If we excuse their poor behavior over and over again, just because they are young, how will they learn to treat people with respect and compassion, as they grow older?

I urge parents to stop this behavior early in a child's life. Say, "No, we don't make fun of others. Life is full of people who are all different. We have to respect everyone. If someone is not nice to you, you can stay away from that person. I want you to understand that you will meet many different people — small, large, tall, short, dark, light — and everyone is a person and we must respect one another."

A parent must teach values to the child. Just as we need to be respectful of our children's feelings, they must learn to be respectful of their friends and classmates. Little by little they're taught that we treat others in a way that we would like to be treated. When a child kicks another child, for example, a parent needs to intervene and say, "We do not kick other people." A parent can say that they are unhappy with the behavior or that it is inappropriate. Eventually a child will learn to control their impulses.

As parents we cannot expect the school to teach our child how to behave. That is our job. The parent is the primary teacher of acceptable behavior and is responsible for helping their children to grow up as reasonable, compassionate and responsible adults.

A child may not like being told that they are not behaving in an appropriate way. However, when a child needs to learn certain behaviors, a parent can present them in such a way that the child will understand that this is a necessary part of parenting.

They may not, and certainly will not, appreciate everything they are told when they are young, but as they get older and I hope, wiser, they will understand that their parents care and want the best for them.

How do I handle my children's chores and responsibilities?

Every parent decides what they expect of their children concerning chores, and helping with daily responsibilities. There is no one "right" way to decide how to handle this issue with your children. Often, I think parents need to look at their children and decide what is reasonable and what would be helpful and educational, and what would be too demanding.

Some parents ask too little; some ask too much. Others fight with their children when the experience of helping out in a family should be a positive one, which helps a child understand he or she is a part of a working unit.

The parent wants to teach a child that people in a family work together and help each other. Even as young as age five, a child should help set the table or clear the dishes, or take out the garbage. Some children get an allowance for their chores — others do not. It varies in families and it is up to the parent to be creative in finding a balance which works for everyone.

I think that children should be introduced to the concept of helping at a very early age. They should be thanked for their efforts and told that you appreciate their help. I like the idea of children helping in the kitchen or with the laundry. The idea that one person is part of a team makes children understand that they need to be thoughtful to others in the family.

They must realize that their parents work hard and that they need to be helpful. It is a lesson that children need to acquire early on in their development.

Sometimes, parents do so much for their children, yet when the parent asks them for some help, the answer is "No," or "I'll do it later."

These children haven't been taught that they are part of a team and that people help each other on a team. These children just expect more and more from their parents without giving back. It is a mistake to keep giving if a child does not give back. You are doing your child a disservice, because they aren't learning to grow up as a helpful, caring person.

We need to help children learn from an early age those certain responsibilities and duties for which they are responsible. This is part of a child's development and a very important lesson that will serve them well in school, in sports and as they become adults.

Life is about learning that we are part of a team in every area of life. The child who learns this early on finds it less difficult to take on duties in their adult lives. The young boy who helps his mother with the dishes might be more receptive to helping his wife in the kitchen and perhaps will be a better husband because he realizes that he is part of a team. Although this may seem simplistic, it is a very important truth.

Going to school for the first time

Going to school for the first time is a landmark event in the lives of a child and their parents. It may be the first time the child is away from the mother for any extended period of time, and vice versa (yes, parents have a difficult time separating as well). Parents need to prepare their child for this day ahead of time. Communication with the child is the cornerstone of making this event a happy and successful experience. The first step is to make sure you are prepared so you can better prepare your child.

You can read books from the library about that first day, and perhaps read a book on the subject to your child.

A thorough discussion of the events that will take place that day is an invaluable time-tested method, which can allay virtually all of your child's fears from the start.

You may tell the child who will be in charge, if they are going on a bus, and who will pick them up and when. It is a time to ask your child to talk about their feelings and what they may be thinking.

They may have concerns that you had not even thought they would have. Do not try to talk your child out of their fears. This is a common mistake. Let the child know that you understand that they may be fearful and that it is okay to have that feeling. Telling the child about someone who is famous, or known for bravery and was afraid of the first day of the school will help them feel more at ease as the child can then identify with that person.

You may tell the child that their day will be full of special times. Further, reminding the child that they can think about another special time or that their parents love them will help the child through the day if and when they feel upset. A child must be told that they can go to the teacher if they need to ask for some help.

When you see your child at the end of the day, be sure to let them tell you every minute detail of the day, and make sure to really pay attention and let them know you are listening. This will reinforce to the child that school is an experience that the family is sharing and that all their thoughts will be accepted.

However, if your child comes home and does not want to share at that moment, do not bombard them with questions — they may need some time and some space. Respect their wishes. At a later time, slowly ask questions so you can see what their day was like. If they seem unhappy or they do not want to speak or they do not want to go to school, the parent must begin to find out what the problem may be.

The child may be shy or there might have been some incident at school that was hurtful. This time of exploring the issues is a beginning for both parents and children to talk and to expressing ideas and concerns. If this dialogue becomes the basis of your relationship, then the child can always come to you when they have a problem and you will then be the major influence in their life.

This is a perfect opportunity to begin building a foundation of communication and trust between parent and child. This is the most wonderful gift we can give our children.

How do we handle an older child's being jealous or resentful of the new baby?

One of the most important times in a child's life is the birth of a sibling. The parents need to prepare the older sibling for the new arrival, yet we know that no amount of preparation can take away a child's feelings as a new sibling arrives.

If the child is verbal, then they can talk about the new baby. It is very important that parents realize that this is a special moment in the older child's life that needs special thoughtfulness from the parents. This is not a time to talk the child out of any of their feelings. It is not the time to tell the child he or she has to love the new baby.

It is a time to help the child experience all their feelings even if it is difficult to hear them. This is such an important moment for everyone. If the parent understands that the older child has just been displaced from being an only child, it may be easier to understand what they may be feeling.

Imagine for yourself if your spouse suddenly brought home a new husband or wife. They calmly explained to you that this new spouse would not take your place, but would be a permanent member of the family, and would be loved just as much as you are, and that of course you must love this new spouse, too.

Even as an adult this idea is very hard to swallow! Imagine being a young child who is used to your full attention and love. Compassion and understanding for the older child are definite musts.

Parents who handle this period with this type of awareness will definitely have an easier time with the older child. If the parent does not understand this period and tries to get the older child to negate their feelings, then trouble begins and it often shows up in school.

If the parent is unaware of the older child's ambivalent feelings then the child will often take these into the school situation. A child may start being more aggressive, or may start wetting again, trying to be like the baby at home. A parent needs to know that this is normal but a sign that the child may need some attention.

The parent who is well versed about what happens when there is a new child will help the older child to make the transition more easily. It is a difficult time and parents must be aware of how important their role is for everyone. If the older child needs some attention, this must be done before there are more problems. Often, I tell parents to spend some special time alone with the older child. Helping the child talk about the new arrival is very important.

Parents need to remember that they may not like hearing everything that the child may say. Be prepared, and be helpful, not defensive. This is no time to tell the child their feelings are wrong. It is a time to listen and find ways to improve the situation. This is a time when mothers may not want to hear that the older child has ambivalent feelings about the baby or that they hate the baby.

Mothers must be prepared to let their children have all their feelings, even though they may be difficult to hear.

If the child is hitting the baby, then the mother must tell the child that they cannot hit the baby, even if they are angry that the baby is here. This is important because this can sometimes happen when there is a new sibling — the older child often becomes more aggressive and the parent usually becomes alarmed. Understanding that this is a natural reaction of the older child's to being usurped from the center of his/her parents' world, the parents can react with love and patience. It is a time when feelings and actions are explained to the child. The child can be made to understand that they can have any feeling, even "bad" ones, about the new baby and the new situation, but they cannot act on the feeling.

In other words, they can be angry at the new baby, but they cannot hit or punch or squeeze the baby. This is a very important explanation because it allows the older child to have their feelings but lets them know they cannot act on them. This is often a time that I tell parents to buy a punching bag for the older child if he/she is too angry.

This is such a crucial point for the older child because if they are told that they cannot have their feelings, what are they to do with all their thoughts and feelings? It makes a person crazy to be told that what they are feeling is not what they are feeling. It is more than unfair; it is dangerous.

Helping them verbalize at this point is a gift that will stay with them forever. I hope that parents who read this understand the importance of helping their children with this transition of becoming a sibling. It is one of the times in the child's life that will forever influence them as they grow and mature. Children whose parents understand the importance of allowing them to have all their feelings will be better able to make the transition to the next part of their existence with ease. They will have the comfort and safety of knowing that their parents love them even when they have negative feelings.

The message then becomes clear — you can have your feelings but you cannot do anything destructive.

This is a wonderful gift to your children. In effect you are saying, "I will listen to your feelings but I will not allow you to hurt your brother or sister." This is an example of saying no to your child, all the while knowing that you are helping them with their impulses.

How do I help my child play alone and be comfortable with being alone?

Too often, parents tell me that their children cannot be alone or that they are always bored. It is hard to believe that with all the toys in this world, any child could ever have that thought. It is true that children always seem to want to have a friend around or want their parents to constantly entertain them.

I've given much thought to this common theme in consulting, and have come up with these ideas. Years ago, when my children were young, there was a playpen which I used every day for a little while when I was in the kitchen or when I was busy. The child sat in the playpen alone with a few toys (I had special playpen toys) and played alone for a little while as I did chores.

This served a multitude of purposes. It gave me time to do things I needed to do and it gave my children an opportunity to play alone with their special toys. In looking back, it was a way for a child to experience a few minutes of being alone every day in a positive way.

Perhaps if the process of being alone starts very early in a child's life, they will become skilled at playing by themselves and learning to be comfortable with the idea that someone is around yet they can be content while playing by themselves.

Yet these days the idea of the playpen seems to be something of the past. Mothers tell me that they do not use them — I wonder why? I think some parents believe that if they use a playpen they are abusing their child in some way — by neglecting them for a moment. Certainly I wouldn't advocate leaving your child in a playpen for an extended period of time, especially if you are not in the room with them.

For a few minutes, even up to an hour, depending on how they are enjoying themselves, this can be an excellent introduction to the idea that it is okay to be alone and it is okay to play alone because I know that mommy or daddy is nearby. Parents need to help their children to be creative in their play if they are alone and learn to be comfortable being alone as there are times when children cannot have playmates or their parents are too busy to play with them.

This is a process that needs to be instituted early in the child's development. It can become a tool throughout childhood to help a child to feel comfortable and happy on his/her own.

How important is eating dinner together as a family?

It is my feeling that this can be an extremely important activity for families to be involved in and could serve as the central family activity around which each member of the family can feel connected to each other and part of the family unit as a whole.

With parents' busy schedule and the fact that many homes have both parents working it is sometimes difficult to get everyone around the dinner table at the same time, but my advice to parents is to make a concerted effort to coordinate this activity. It is a wonderful feeling to have everyone at dinner discussing what went on during each person's day. Often, if we begin this activity early on it becomes an important family tradition or ritual which will become part of the teenager's life.

Many children have told me that dinnertime was an important time to them: a time to exchange ideas, thoughts, experiences and discuss problems or concerns and get help and advice.

For families where getting everyone together for dinner is just not feasible then I suggest setting aside a special family time on the weekend.

Have a special breakfast Saturday or Sunday morning, with everyone present, or choose some other time that is set aside and special to everyone in the family. Also ensure that it happens so it becomes an important part of the family's interaction.

How do you deal with taking your child shopping and not buying them everything?

Saying "no" when you are in the toy aisle is a very important no. If possible, you can decide in advance to allow your child to get one toy — something reasonable. When they ask for another, you can remind them, "Today we get this toy and the next time we go shopping we can get another." This teaches the child that one toy is reasonable — and that they can wait for next time for more. If mom or dad buys something next time they know that the promise was kept. This is a good message for the child. It teaches the child about patience. Children have trouble tolerating frustration. If they act up in a store — take them out. Do not reward behavior that is unacceptable. If your child cannot sit and shop with you, do not bring them along.

How do I handle a situation when I am disappointed in my child's behavior?

When we are raising children, it is inevitable that there will be times when our children behave in a way that really shocks us. When something like this happens, often the parent cannot understand why the child has behaved in such an inappropriate manner. I usually ask parents to think about if the deed is age appropriate. If it is, then the parent must understand that the child needs to be taught that they cannot write on the walls or kick people or bite or make fun of another child, for a few examples.

Parents need to sit down with their child and explain that some behaviors are inappropriate while other behaviors are acceptable. A child does not know these things until the parent educates them.

Accusing them in anger, or demanding to know what is wrong with them is not helpful and is really not the issue. They are children and need to learn acceptable behavior.

Some problems are more serious than others. Teenagers who steal need more than education. They need to be told how you feel about this kind of deed — how it is against the law and morally wrong. The parent must think of a punishment that is appropriate and follow through with it.

Beyond punishment and explanation about the behavior to your child, you need to look at why the child is behaving in this way. What is happening in their life at that particular moment? Is the child in need of attention? To a child, positive or negative attention still equals attention. A parent needs to look closely at the problem and figure out solutions. A parent should look closely at behavior that is inappropriate and pay attention. You need to remember that a small problem may turn into a large one if you assume that your child will simply outgrow the bad behavior.

In helping countless parents over twenty years, I have found that looking at what you want for your children helps in determining the best way for you to help your children grow up to be responsible adults.

What do I do when my child is not doing his or her schoolwork?

Children often start doing poorly in school as a reaction to some issue in their life. There might be a friendship or relationship that is breaking up or they may be feeling upset about some family problem. They might have a problem focusing on their work. They may be feeling peer pressure. Often, it is hard to figure out but it is important to communicate with your child to find out what is causing them to not do their work.

Only after discussing the issues, can the parent know what can or should be done. It can be a simple issue or it can be more complicated.

Sometimes a child just needs a little attention. The parent needs to figure out how to help the child if they need help or how to push the child if they need some direction. Each child is different and in looking at issues with children, one has to remember that what works with one child may not work for another, even if they are siblings.

Problems do not go away. You can begin the process of helping your child by telling them that you are concerned. Be proactive in your approach. Fairness is very important. Set limits on TV watching or use of computers or, if age appropriate, on driving the car. These are subjective limits that depend totally on what you as the parents feel will be best in this particular situation.

Often, children know what they need and will be able to tell you — they can be part of the solution. Stay focused on the issue, not on several others that you may be thinking of at that time. The child or teenager should know your concerns and should know also that you are not going to give up.

If a tutor is needed, get that help immediately. If you are finding that your involvement in the homework is unproductive, then remove yourself from the scene. Let someone else be involved. This is a time to look at the problem and find solutions. They may be simpler than you think.

Sometimes a child may just need your attention and sitting with them for a short period of time to get them started is a quick solution that often works. Even if the problem is more complex, there are solutions. Creativity is an essential part of raising a child in today's world. Thinking about various solutions is important and lets your child know that you are always thinking of improving the situation. A child who knows that you are not going to give up, no matter how hard it is, will feel secure and more confident, knowing that their parents are going to work on the issue.

Really, a problem with homework is no different than any other problem. It is like finding the right key for the lock. Children need to know that they can talk to the parent and be involved in the solution of the problem. They need the comfort of knowing they can turn to you.

How do I know how much help my child needs with their homework?

Some children are self-starters who come home, sit down and finish their work without any help from their parents. Some may need a gentle reminder, while others need their parents to sit with them and give them support and a push. It is always important to remember that children are different and that what may work with one sibling may not work for another.

They should be helped to become independent so that they can do their work on their own. However, even if this is the goal — the question is how to achieve the goal. Usually it needs as assessment by the parent, who will decide how much help is needed — how much to push or which combination will work. Parents need to be aware at all times of their child's strengths and weaknesses. It makes parenting much simpler.

Ask your child if they would like help. If your child needs help, it is up to you to decide what is the best plan. Sometimes children can help in devising the plan. If your child is not a self-starter, figure out how much time you need to sit with your child, if they need you to be involved in the assignment or if they just need to know you are there. Often if the parents are working outside the home, a child may just need some attention. As a parent, you should try to figure out what is the right combination of support and attention.

If the parent feels too frustrated, it is often better to add a tutor or a homework helper. If one solution does not work, try another until you find the winning combination.

How do I handle my child's temper tantrums?

Children need to discharge their tensions just like adults do. Many children do not have the language skills to express themselves. Instead, they just scream or cry until they get the attention of the parent. Although parents usually get very upset when they see their child out of control, they need to see the outburst as a means of releasing tension. It is important for the child to see that the parent is in control — however, screaming back at your child is not modeling behavior for them. Staying calm and telling your child that you will be in the next room and they can come and get you when they are finished is one way to handle a tantrum.

The child then calms him/herself and knows when this happens, that you will be waiting in the other room. When parents do this, the child eventually gets the message that they are not going to get their way just because they are screaming.

It also allows them to calm down and then find the parent. It is paramount that parents remain in control when their child is out of control. Two members of a family out of control is a recipe for disaster. Parents need to help children to express themselves so that the child can then tell the parent what they are feeling.

If the child is hurt or is upset about something, you can try to hold them and comfort them. However this is different from the typical tantrum where the child is just frustrated and needs some time to calm down. At all times in the parenting process, we need to be aware that our children are looking to us for guidance — if we are often out of control — how can our children learn the idea of being in control from us?

If we show them that we can tolerate some frustration without losing control, then it is a clear message that they can do the same.

What do I do when my child is exhibiting aggressive behavior?

First, the parent must try to understand what is happening in the child's life. Sometimes the child becomes more aggressive after the birth of another child in the family. Children need help in verbalizing all their thoughts and parents need to listen and help their child process the myriad of feelings that accompany the arrival of a new sibling.

If the child is becoming more aggressive without an obvious explanation, then the parents must try to be detectives who are on a mission to find clues.

Ask yourself these questions:

- a) *Is the behavior only at home or is it also at school?*
- b) *Is something going on in school that might be triggering the behavior?*
- c) *Is the child frustrated with friends?*
- d) *Is the child having an internal emotional conflict?*

Parents can sit down with the child and ask if there is a problem. Often, children can verbalize what may be going on. If they can't, then the parent needs to monitor the situation. The parent needs to tell the child that the aggressive behavior has to stop and make the child part of the solution. How can a child stop the behavior? Well sometimes they can be made to stop with incentives or sometimes they stop with discipline, which means something they like gets taken away.

Sometimes, they can stop when they have verbalized what is causing them to act this way. The parent may need to give the child some extra attention, which sometimes works. The parent needs to be creative. If the parent cannot get to the bottom of the problem, some professional help may be required. Whatever the case is, parents need to look at the issues involved and think — I need to fix this — how can I fix it or do I need some help? If help is needed, it should be looked at as a positive step.

With this type of mind-set, whenever a problem gets to be too difficult, help can be sought. This might be very short-term and yet may be something the family does from time to time to keep everything flowing smoothly.

Why is it important to model a healthy lifestyle for our children?

Parents often come into my office quite concerned when their children are overeating and gaining weight. The child wants to eat junk food instead of dinner — what does the parent say or do? They often give in to their child instead of saying no and possibly having a very angry child on their hands. If the parent can help the child understand what foods are healthful and which foods are going to make them gain weight, the child will begin to have the awareness that all foods are not the same.

We must realize that children see other kids bring junk food to school and it is difficult for parents to teach children what they should or should not eat. Parents who eat well and stay fit are more likely to have children who are fit. You don't have to embark on a full-scale workout regime. You can ride a bike or jump rope or go for a walk. Children need to see their parents being active.

Parents who are active and fit model this behavior for their children. We cannot help a child be fit, if we continue to overeat and be unfit ourselves. Children should be helped at all times, because they are always vulnerable to teasing when they are overweight and often have difficulty participating in sports.

In today's society, children need to know which foods are good for them. That it is important that they exercise as parens reinforce what is expected of them.

What children learn very quickly is that other children can be cruel toward them when they are overweight. It is something so hurtful to children, I hear about this all the time. Children walk into my office absolutely devastated by a comment from another child about their weight. It is much easier to acquire good habits when we are young. Adults have a hard time taking pounds off. We must help children stay healthy and fit when they are young and impressionable.

Why is feeling positive about their body image so important for our children?

In today's world, thin is in and heavy is unacceptable. Children can be very hurtful to each other, which is one reason that heavy children feel excluded not only from sports but also they find themselves on the outside of many social circles. Some children at the age of seven are already talking about being fat and needing to be on a diet.

The magazines focus on being slim — to the point of emaciation. Girls are especially vulnerable but it is also beginning to affect boys. Kids are talking about being fat instead of talking about kid stuff. As in all things, children learn through example. They hear their parents talking about what to eat, which diet plan to try, which exercise program to pursue. Children are aware of the focus on being thin and beautiful.

If there is a weight issue in the family, the parent can talk to the child and discuss problems and issues of weight, diet and exercise. I think these discussions can lead to greater understanding between parent and child. If you see a problem, bring it up for discussion. Often, because of the sensitivity of the subject, everyone may be afraid to address the issue. If the topic is avoided, then children might respond to the perceived weight issue in a more destructive manner.

Kids who are active and fit are not only practicing good health habits but are better able to maintain a positive self-esteem. A child who feels good about him/herself is a child who can say no to drugs, alcohol and peer pressure. It is in the best interest of our children to help them feel confident and positive about themselves. Parents must understand how society is focused on appearance and that 'thin is in'. Also, being overweight can be a problem for girls and for boys. The boy who is not picked for soccer or the girl who looks different than the other girls because she is overweight can begin feelings of discrimination even at a very early age. When children tease each other, it can be devastating for the child being teased.

Often, parents do not realize how a child feels when they are not picked for games at recess or they are told that they cannot join the group. Children often keep this type of hurt to themselves because they are too embarrassed or feel hopeless. Often, the children left out are consumed with feeling bad about themselves and therefore their work or their moods may be affected. The parent may find a child who is short-tempered but does not understand why. Sometimes parents have to be detectives to find out what is wrong.

Much of this pain and distress can be avoided at the outset by teaching our children, though modeling and communication, to live a healthful lifestyle.

Why has the peer group become so important?

The peer group has always had importance in any child's life, but somehow it has become even more important than ever. Children want to be accepted and get approval. This seeming endless need for peer approval has become great that you have to look at many issues when examining this issue.

Children come to my office talking about their friends more than about their families and I wonder why this has become such a source of conversation.

The idea that children feel that their parents do not understand them comes up all the time. So, if their parents do not understand or are too busy working or not paying attention, has the peer group become the place where the child then gets validation for their feelings?

If the child feels that the parents are not listening, then the peer group becomes the place for relief, comfort and advice. Well, what happens if that particular group is involved with drugs or alcohol? Is the child then more susceptible to getting involved with destructive behaviors?

The answer is a resounding yes. If a child is not turning to the parent, then whom are they talking to and what will happen? If the peer group happens to be one where experimenting is not going on, then the child is safer. It is an issue that parents need to look at early in their child's development.

Parents need to ask themselves, "How are we going to prevent some of the problems that are obviously there and how can we look at some of these suggestions in this book as a way of preventing major problems? If my child is worried about being fat and I am not listening as a parent — will the child then emulate a peer who now has found a way of controlling their weight? These are a few thoughts for the parent who wants to understand parenting in this difficult era.

As parents we can simplify the issues if we are looking at the ideas of communication and modeling as the core of our parenting. Yes, it seems to me that, as a parent, I would want to address issues before they become problems. The other issue for parents to understand is simple.

Children want to feel accepted. They want the right sneakers, the right jeans and the right look. Parents need to understand that these thoughts are normal and that we must accept that our children have them. We cannot tell them they are selfish or that it is unimportant. We must give them the feeling that we understand what they may be going through even if we find it unusual or different from our childhood.

Often, parents say you do not need that or you are too selfish — you want everything your friends have. Yes, that may be true but it would be more productive to let them know that it may be difficult to get all the things their friends have. You can let them know that you can feel their hurt when they have less but that it is part of life to know that everyone is different and that they may have more than some and less than others.

Even if you need to explain the entire issue of money and your financial circumstances, that is better than telling them they are ridiculous or they are selfish. There are so many things to ask for in this world, that it is hard to be a child in a world where there is so much out there advertised as necessary to be accepted. It is also hard to be a parent who has to say yes and no to the many things that children ask for.

That is the reason for this book — a look into a different world than the one we had. I hope this book will give you some of the coping skills to help you become a better parent, and to provide your children with a better chance to grow up as productive, happy, compassionate members of our society.

What happens when your teenager wants to come out to dinner at a restaurant wearing clothes that you disapprove of?

This often happens. Teenagers want to express themselves. Sometimes a parent can say, "No, you cannot wear this out to dinner. We are going to a nice restaurant. I know you like these clothes but can you do me a favor for one night?"

Last week Dina wanted to go out to dinner with her parents. She was in my office and she and her mother were negotiating a dress code. I finally said, "Dina, your mother really needs you to dress appropriately for the restaurant — can you put your dress code aside for one night?" She finally said okay, but only for tonight.

What do you do with a teenager and their messy room?

Parents do different things depending on how important a clean room is to them. If the parents can tolerate the mess and close the door — it can be that simple. Teenagers have a million ways to excuse the condition of their room. "It's my room! Why do I have to keep it clean?" Sometimes parents make deals with their kids. Often parents cannot tolerate what the teenager is saying.

If we can look at it as a phase we can be happier about the situation. If the teenager is doing well in school and in every other area — why can't we just overlook the condition of their room? If the teenager is doing poorly in other areas and their room is a mess — it is probably a message. Parents need to check out what the message is.

Personally, I was happy when the kids were doing well in school. I gave up on the mess. I "chose my battles" and a clean room was not one of them. Parents need to communicate with their child. Sometimes the parent tells the child, "Look, I am having a problem with the mess. Can I help you? Can you do this for me? Can I pay you? Can I bribe you? What can I do, or should I just look at this as a phase?"

One of my clients told his mother to give it up. Another client told his mother that it was their form of rebellion. Kids can be funny and each child is different. What can the parent tolerate?

What if I suspect my child is involved in substance abuse?

The number of teens using drugs has increased and the age of onset of use has decreased to the point where many children are using drugs before reaching puberty. The effects of drug use before puberty are pervasive and include growth delay and brain damage. Unfortunately, some kids today accept drug use as the norm.

Unlike when we were raised, today's child is exposed to illicit drugs at a much earlier age and therefore the problems are greater than they have ever been. How can a parent try to shield their child even at a very young age?

In studying this situation, it seems that the child who has a sense of self-worth and feels good about him/herself is less likely to get involved in drugs. For a child, drugs can be an escape from reality, or a friend that they can count on. It is a dependency that grows and grows. Children who have self-esteem issues are more likely to get involved with drugs because they want the approval of their peer group. Others who feel good about themselves and their self-worth will be better able to say no when they are faced with drugs as they grow up.

If the parent realizes right from the start that the child needs limits, discipline, love and respect, the child will probably be less likely to look at the peer group for their approval. They will have a relationship with their parents which gives them the feelings of belonging and acceptance, which is what they will seek from the peer group if they can't find it at home. The parent needs to help the child develop good social skills and the ability to manage their interpersonal relationships. Children who feel good about themselves often are able to say no. They can manage their peer group without feeling they must say yes.

A parent needs to educate the child about drugs while also educating them about the peer group pressures that they are going to face as they grow up. This along with good communications between parent and child lessens the peer group influence. The issue of trust, listening and dialogue in families is the best way to strengthen the child's ability to stand strong and say no. Being able to say no to peer pressure is the strength we need to help our children develop.

In looking at this problem, it is wise as parents to think about these issues at a very early age and say I want my children to feel good about themselves right from the start, so how can I ensure this will happen?

Some important clues if you think your child may be involved with drugs or alcohol are as follows:

- Change in sleeping patterns
- Change in eating patterns
- Fatigue, loss of energy
- Loss of interest or pleasure in activities
- Feelings of worthlessness
- Feelings of guilt
- Recurring thoughts of death and suicide

If your child is exhibiting some of these signs, talk to your doctor or mental health professional.

The problem of increased drug and alcohol use is an issue that schools, parents and elected officials all think about, talk about and are looking at solutions for. TV is being flooded with ads about brain damage — brains are being fried. This is unfortunately not the issue. The problem is much greater than showing fried brains on TV, although this is a well-intentioned effort to dramatize the seriousness of the problem and its possible consequences.

What is driving these children to drug and alcohol use at such early ages? Although there are many reasons — one of the ways we can help the generation that is growing up at this point is to help them feel positive about themselves and their self-worth. When they are then faced with peer pressure and have a choice of saying yes or no, they might be able to feel strong enough to say no and tolerate the feeling of not being part of a group.

The child who feels strong in their convictions can face the peer group and know that they have done the right thing. They can come to their parents with the problems and know that they have in them allies. These are issues that need to be addressed at an early age. Let us teach our children that they are important, they are worthy and that they have the power to be the leaders, not the followers.

How do we raise a reasonable child?

It is easy to say we are going to give into reasonable requests as we raise our children. Often the parent needs to understand what is reasonable. If we begin this philosophy early on in a child's development they begin to know what is reasonable because they have been trained early in life. What happens if you have given in so much that your child is very demanding and you are at the point of being quite frustrated?

You can always change the way you parent. You are not tied to one way of handling a problem. If you feel you are giving in too much, you can decide, with a united approach from both of you as parents, to create a plan where you will say "yes" to what is reasonable and "no" to what is not. It may be difficult and it should not be done all at once, but you can discuss with the child that there will be some disagreements but whatever you were doing was not working. Children might not like it but it is true that arguing is not desirable. You can say "We are fighting and something is not working, and there will be some changes." Parents cannot be in denial about anything. They must constantly evaluate the home situation. If you think something is wrong, then you must be open-minded enough to think that change is necessary. If it can be done within the family that is okay. If outside help is needed, that should always be an option.

It is up to you as the parent to realize that in changing your plan your child may have a reaction. If you are used to indulging your child, he or she will not be happy with the change. It has to be done with great thought and selflessness. This is often the point at which people contact me. Taking back power is not easy — it is very hard work.

What do we do to help our children feel good about themselves as people?

I think this is all part of the parenting plan. It should always be a plan of acknowledging behavior that is responsible. It is complimenting something the child has achieved. Do not attack them when you are displeased with some of their behavior. Address their behavior, not their essence. Don't scream, yell or respond negatively to their demands even if they are outrageous. Remember always, that children who like themselves do not have to depend on their peer group for validation. Remember always to think about the family's situation in order to come up with a plan. Plans need customizing depending on circumstances. If a nanny or baby-sitter is taking care of a child she must be aware of what and how you expect her to deal with your child. If someone is yelling at your child when you are away eight hours a day you will need to factor firing this person into your plan. As long as you keep an open mind, a sense of creativity and look to this book for suggestions, I expect the parenting road will be smoother for you.

Ten things <u>never</u> to say to your children:

- *What's wrong with you?*
- *You are so selfish.*
- *You are lazy.*
- *How could you be so stupid?*
- *Your sister/brother is smarter than you are.*
- *You are so clumsy.*
- *Why did you do something so stupid?*
- *You look fat.*
- *Your clothes are disgusting.*
- *I hate your friends.*

Although these are thoughts that the parent may have, these are all attacks. If our goal is to make children feel good about themselves, these are words that are not only hurtful, but can be very damaging to a small child or even an older child.

Rather than focusing on these perceived shortcomings, this kind of approach will instead result in drawing the focus to you. You become the "bad parent" who says mean and hurtful things. You will shut down the lines of communication by attacking. Instead, try to keep the focus on positive ways to change — on the issues, not on the child.

Some of the ways these thoughts can be verbalized in a more positive manner include:

- *I realize this work is difficult. Is there something we can do to help you?*
- *I know you would like another toy, but right now we cannot buy anything else.*
- *Mom and dad are not happy when you act this way.*
- *The homework seems difficult. Would you like some help?*
- *Do we need to work on helping you with your weight?*
- *What can we do to help you?*

The essence of parenting is to guide, not to attack. Children often do things that convince us that they are children. If we are unhappy about something, we can tell them. For example, "Mom and dad are not happy when you hit your sister. We do not hit." This is preferable to yelling at them for their aggressive tendencies.

Yelling should be reserved for a moment when they are about to run into the street, or they are about to do something that might prove very dangerous. Talking to a child about their behavior in such a way that they listen without becoming defensive is key to good communication.

Yelling at them when they are out of control just shows them that you are out of control, too. Because modeling is a cornerstone of parenting, my suggestion is that if you have a problem with something your child has done, let them know why and how you feel.

Stay calm, listen and guide. Do not accuse before you know the facts.

Then, if necessary, find a punishment that suits the situation. If you do not think that it requires a punishment, then figure out how you are going to handle the situation. Sometimes parents can let their child know they are disappointed. Every situation is different and requires a different solution.

What happens when we keep saying yes?

Overindulgence leads to more unreasonable requests, which leads to more tension between parent and child. Children who keep asking for more and then get what they want feel entitled to more and more. The parent then gets angry at them for who they have become. A cycle has been created that now requires major intervention.

The child who has been accustomed to getting everything, cannot understand why the parent is angry. The parent calls them demanding, ungrateful and selfish among other things and this only adds to the tension. The child is angry with the parent; the parent is angry with the child. When the child finally hears a no, they get angry with the parent because they really feel entitled. They get into a habit of being more and more demanding. Parents get mad at them for being outrageous. The parent is angry at the child for being so demanding, yet this is the only thing that the child has learned. "I get what I ask for even if it is unreasonable, so why should I stop?" They do not understand why the parent calls them ungrateful after being trained to get whatever they ask for.

So what started as wanting to give your child everything you did not have, has become a disaster. Yes, we wanted to be good parents, so we said yes and now we have created a situation where the child only knows what he or she wants without a thought for us. How could this have happened? It was easy; we did not know it was happening because it was so gradual. We just gave without any expectations from our child... so what was the child to learn? Yes, they learned "I am the center of the universe and everything revolves around me."

It is a message they learn quickly just like the one when they were babies getting up in the middle of the night and the parent kept giving them a bottle. How quickly they learn to get up every hour! It's the same quick message and it's hard to stop.

We cannot be angry at our children for what we have created, we have to take some responsibility, and we must change our direction. First, we must calm down, and truly understand the problem. Only then can we make changes. Talking to our partners or someone we respect can be a beginning.

Charts, Graphs and Helpful Hints

10 REASONS PARENTS SHOULD PRAISE OR REWARD THEIR CHILDREN

1. Exhibiting behavior that demonstrates good morals
2. Being kind
3. Acting responsibly
4. Getting good grades
5. Using good judgment
6. Working hard
7. Asking for advice
8. Exhibiting sportsmanship
9. Showing respect
10. Acting reasonably

10 WARNING SIGNS THAT YOUR CHILD MAY BE FACING CONFLICT OR TROUBLE

1. Increase in aggressive behavior
2. Depressed or unhappy disposition
3. Antisocial behavior
4. Inability to keep friends
5. Lack of energy
6. Change in weight or eating habits
7. Change in school performance
8. Change in level of communication
9. Change in sleep patterns
10. Change in appearance

10 COMMON THINGS FOR PARENTS TO SAY "NO" TO

1. Jumping on furniture
2. Hitting and or pushing
3. Making fun of others
4. Excessive watching of TV or videos
5. Excessive consumption of junk foods
6. Excessive hours playing with the computer or video games
7. Excessive demands for toys
8. Driving without a license
9. Underage drinking
10. Attending unsupervised parties

10 WAYS TO PRAISE YOUR CHILD

Words of praise can often be quite powerful and hard to live up to for the child. Parents say "You are wonderful" or "You are so great" or the ever-popular "You are so beautiful!" These words can lead to the child's being broken-hearted, when he or she does not receive them, or having an inflated representation of him/herself. You can praise a child's actions, and should. Actions are qualifiable and are not up for comparison.

What you can say ...

- Good job
- Thumbs up
- Mom and dad are proud of your behavior.
- We are proud of your sportsmanship on the field.
- I am proud of the way you showed respect to your teachers.
- We are proud of the way you are acting, taking responsibility with your work.
- I am happy that you asked for help with this situation, it shows good judgment.
- Those were good grades. We are proud of you and YOU should be proud of yourself. You worked hard and it shows.... .
- I was happy to see that you did not make fun of that child because it shows good character. Character is very important in life. *(THIS is your opportunity to talk about the importance of morals.)*
- We are happy you told us the truth. You should never be afraid to tell us the truth.

THINGS TO REMEMBER

THE YOUNGER CHILD

Use distraction for the younger child instead of saying no to everything.

Do not attack them when they do something wrong... deal with the act or the behavior.

Remember your child's temperment.

Take into consideration your own temperament and the one of your spouse.

Understand the stage your child is going through.

Know what is reasonable and what is not... the parenting plan.

Try to be creative, reflective and consistent.

Praise the child for positive behaviors or actions.

Stay away from the words *great* or *wonderful*... they are hard to live up to when you are a kid.

Work as a team with your partner.

If you are a single parent discuss issues with someone you respect.

THINGS TO REMEMBER

GRADE SCHOOL AND THE TEENAGE YEARS

Remember the media and peer pressure as major influences.

Be proactive not reactive.

Praise when you can for any positive acts.

Be honest when you talk about the dangers of life.

Know your facts when you speak about drugs, alcohol and smoking.

Don't tell them their feelings are wrong.

Create the bonds so they are in place when the turbulent teenage years come.

Do not attack their friends... it may not work.

Speak with authority when you are worried about their safety.

Stay calm even when you want to scream.

Talk to a friend when you are overwhelmed.

Stay focused on the issues at hand... do not let your child sidetrack you to some other issue so that you lose your focus.

If your child needs more than you can offer... find help.

Have faith and hope that you will deal with any issues that come up.

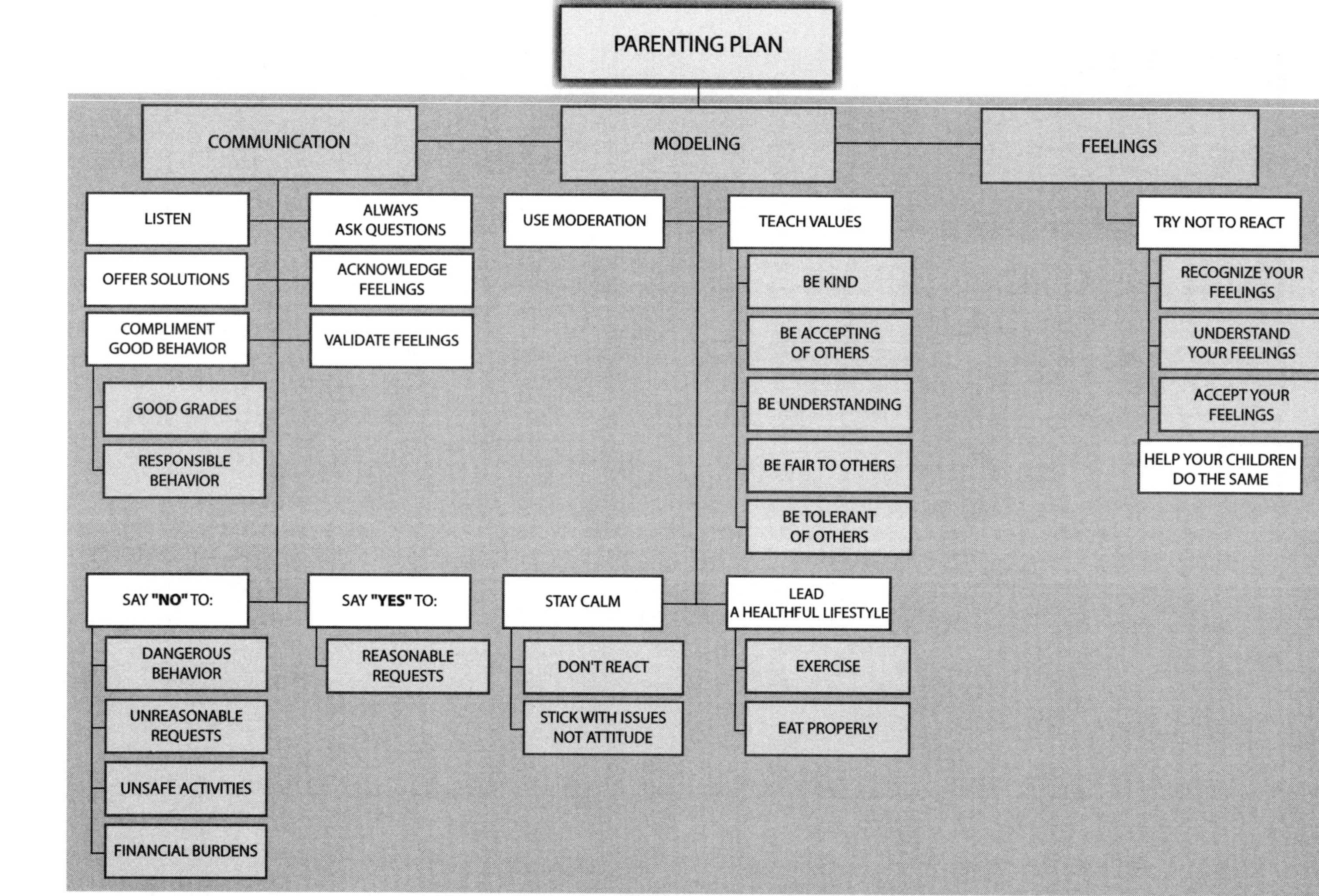
PARENTING PLAN
COMMUNICATION
MODELING
FEELINGS
LISTEN
ALWAYS ASK QUESTIONS
OFFER SOLUTIONS
ACKNOWLEDGE FEELINGS
COMPLIMENT GOOD BEHAVIOR
VALIDATE FEELINGS
GOOD GRADES
RESPONSIBLE BEHAVIOR
SAY "NO" TO:
DANGEROUS BEHAVIOR
UNREASONABLE REQUESTS
UNSAFE ACTIVITIES
FINANCIAL BURDENS
SAY "YES" TO:
REASONABLE REQUESTS
USE MODERATION
TEACH VALUES
BE KIND
BE ACCEPTING OF OTHERS
BE UNDERSTANDING
BE FAIR TO OTHERS
BE TOLERANT OF OTHERS
STAY CALM
DON'T REACT
STICK WITH ISSUES NOT ATTITUDE
LEAD A HEALTHFUL LIFESTYLE
EXERCISE
EAT PROPERLY
TRY NOT TO REACT
RECOGNIZE YOUR FEELINGS
UNDERSTAND YOUR FEELINGS
ACCEPT YOUR FEELINGS
HELP YOUR CHILDREN DO THE SAME

Letters From The Parents

Since my daughter was an easygoing child, who was eager to please those close to her, I never dreamed that I would suddenly be facing problems of great magnitude with her in her teen years. It was devastating to watch her self-esteem fall along with her grades and friendships while her unhappiness, inability to cope and her weight rose. I had no idea where I went wrong as her mother. As she plummeted into depression, I followed.

Norma helped me to realize that my daughter's problems arose because she had never experienced a 'No' at home. I did not parent by setting limits, rather allowed my daughter to self-discipline. She had no role model for setting limits with others in her life. She pleased others at her expense. I had to change my parenting so the she could learn to reclaim control of her relationships and her life.

I am grateful for the redirection. My daughter is a new and better woman. So am I.

~ E.K

Working with Norma has enabled our family to achieve a calmer household. As parents, we have learned to act towards our daughter in the same way we want her to act towards us. She has helped us create a "plan" for dealing with difficult situations. Thanks to Norma, we have stopped yelling and screaming in our house.

~ B.B

Norma has been an invaluable coach, listener and advisor to my husband, my five-year-old daughter and myself. She has taught us skills necessary to address the needs of our exceptionally bright and very intense child. We have learned to be calm and patient with our selves to demonstrate to our daughter how to handle her own challenges. Norma has been dedicated and determined to see our family through even the most difficult times. She is always available to us, which has been a useful tool. With her guidance, our focus on parenting frustrations has been redirected to a focus to guiding our bright and strong-willed daughter to a successful future.

~ M.C

To write a tribute to Norma Ross on the publication of her wonderful book is akin to thanking our parents for guiding us through life until that first day of college. Simply stated - I could not have done either as successfully or as smoothly without both my parents and Norma!

Personally, there is undoubtedly no greater joy in my life than being a dad, while at many times I needed a source to go to for answers that did not come naturally. Having Norma Ross in my corner, I knew how to cope with anything that arose in my job of being a dad - the only job that you do not interview for and does not come with any sort of reference guide or instruction book - that is until now!

~ D.K

Letters From The Children

Therapy is a wonderful thing, and I believe everyone should get some. I started going to therapy so I could deal with my parents' divorce. Through the years I have been able to work out family problems, school problems, friend problems, and any other problems that arose. My therapist is someone that I can talk to without fear of judgment or consequences. Many kids have a hard time telling their parents things because they are afraid of what their parents might do about it. For those kids, therapy provides an outlet for any pent up feelings that they can't share with anyone else.

I have learned a lot from going to therapy. I have learned to express myself to others and not keep my feelings inside. I have become adept at analyzing both myself and other people. This is a great help, especially since all of my friends come to me for advice. I have come to learn that the best advice is the kind you come up with yourself. Therefore when I am trying to help a friend through a problem, I ask them questions that allow them to come to their own conclusion. I learned how to do this from my therapist.

I used to be embarrassed about going to therapy. I felt people would think I was crazy and unstable. Well, I believe that everyone in life is crazy and unstable, and it is those who go to therapy that have any chance of overcoming that craziness and instability. I am glad that my parents had the foresight to send me to someone I could talk to freely, and I have learned not to be embarrassed by going.

Therapy has helped me immensely, and I would not be the stable person I was today if I didn't go. Someone once asked me if there were one thing to make this world better what would it be? At the time I had no idea. But now that I look back at my 18 years of life I have come up with an answer. Go to therapy!!!

~ An 18-year-old boy

Teenagers are more self-regulated than one would think; I feel that I am able to make such a statement being that I have been one for a good 5 years of my life. For the most part, we know what we want, what we need and have some vague idea of how to get there ourselves. This characteristic of our kind is somewhat disguised by the way we dress, act and by our parents' vivid memories of us as defenseless little babies. On the other hand, despite this wealth of ability we posses we also need guidance despite our "I don't need them for anything attitude." We are very complex entities, we know what we want, need to be guided, but don't want our parents help for anything. Therapy helps us get it all. We not only get the guidance we need and what we want, with in reason, but develop the negotiation skills to do so. Whether it be the privilege of driving an automobile or a later curfew, therapy serves and a neutral "battle ground" or more accurately, "playing field" where parents and children can relate to one another on the same level.

~ A 17 year old boy

I think it is safe to say that I am the world's biggest therapy advocate. I am 18 years old and have been in therapy for about 3.5 years. You would think that I ended up in therapy because I was a juvenile delinquent and my parents dragged me there to make some sense out of my behavior but that is just not the case.
I am a straight A student, am involved in many extra curricular activities, and am moral, honest and independent. Therefore it is

sufficed to say my parents did an excellent job raising me. However, 3.5 years ago I begged them to take me to therapy. You see, emotionally there was just something off. My parents and I had some major communication problems. Then I realized while my parents had some how made me turn out so great, it was now my responsibility to in turn raise my parents.

Therapy was my translator. It allowed me to communicate my needs to my parents without being misunderstood. We were all able to set rules and guidelines for each other. Today I feel very close to my family. A lot of the resent and animosity I felt towards them is gone. I am going off to college with a feeling of security knowing that my family is behind me and will support me in my life.

I feel the need to continue my counseling because it keeps me up to date with my feelings. It allows me to share every good and bad thing I must deal with. Therapy provides me with an impartial forum to voice my thoughts, opinions, and grievances. I am truly thankful for the way my family has turned out.

~ An 18-year-old girl

One night this year I couldn't sleep. I took out my diary and decided to read it. I read over the year that I was in sixth grade. The person who wrote those things couldn't have been me, but it was. I didn't realize up until that point how troubled I was. I sounded like, if I didn't get help, I would have ended up in an institution. But I did get help. Luckily for me my mother realized I had some problems that needed attention. She took me to a Family Therapist. Back then I thought those sessions were normal, that I was going just to be here. Looking back I thought I was normal, that I had no problems. Going to all those sessions really showed me that I needed help. Being with a therapist is a lot easier than confiding in a parent. When you talk to a therapist you know that whatever you say does not leave the room. Also, the therapist is very support-

ive. A parent may not understand your need for help. All I know is that if I did not get the help I needed I would be a very different person today. I would have sunken deeper into my troubles and would have had a harder time coming back. The help I have received saved my sanity. I still go to my therapist every once in a while to hash over the latest problems or the good things. Right now, I can say that I am very thankful to my therapist, the wonderful author of this book.

~ A 14 years old girl

Sometimes I did not tell my mom certain things because I felt uncomfortable. You never know whether she was going to be mad or sad. But in my life my mom is the biggest supporter. I feel good when I talk to my counselor because I can fully express myself and be able to take things off my chest.

~ A 12 year old boy

Independence. Before "sex, drugs, and rock & roll" it is the first item on a budding teenager's list of things to acquire. However, the need for independence exceeds the actual abilities of the teenager to show Independence. One of the reasons a teen does not tell his or her parents certain things they have done or feelings they have is because those feelings and actions may jeopardize or eliminate any independence the teenager may have. Growing up as a teenager, I was more than certain I was going to smoke pot one way or another. When I did for the first time with my friend on the roof of his building, a new window opened for me.
That window being the entrance way for the life of a druggie. When I began to use it more and more I began to see it become a problem, and the fact that my parents would severely punish me had I

admitted my usage created a no win situation for me to discuss my "problem". What Norma did for me was create a platform on which to discuss my usage of pot honestly and openly with my parents. This would allow me to discuss the facets of using pot and eventually come to a logical conclusion that would benefit me more than if my parents were to punish me. Therapy allows a teen to come to a conclusion by his or her self while the discipline of parents only gives the teen a conclusion on the terms of the parents. In this fragile time for children, a teen must learn to figure things out by themselves to eventually become a well-adjusted person, something counseling can do for a teenager, and something Norma has done for me. For that I thank her.

~ An 18-year-old boy

SMART PARENTING
S O L U T I O N S

Thank you for reading my book. I hope it will empower you on your parenting journey.

If you have any questions, please feel free to contact me:

Tel: (914) 428-1555
Fax: (914) 428-6573
Web: http://www.smartparentingsolutions.com
E-mail: norross98@aol.com

Mail: Smart Parenting Solutions
4 Martine Avenue, Suite 1618
White Plains, New York, 10606

For more information on Smart Parenting Solutions and our educational seminars, programs and services visit: http://www.smartparentingsolutions.com

About The Author

For the last 20 years Norma Ross has been consulting with individuals, parents, couples, children and families on the issues they face on a day-to-day basis. A formally trained psychoanalyst, her specialty has been empowering parents to take control of their children and families. Her practice has evolved from psychoanalytic therapy to parent/family consulting. Through her practical, solution-oriented approach, she helps parents and children deal with sibling rivalry, divorce and step families, school performance, drugs, peer pressure, body image, learning disabilities and behavioral problems, to name a few.

Norma Ross is the President of Smart Parenting Solutions, a consultation firm that she founded to help expand her consultation based parenting practice. Smart Parenting Solutions is fueled by a team of professionals in the areas of psychiatry, psychology, drug and alcohol addictions, eating disorders, medicine, pediatrics, etc. to consult parents, children, families, teachers, professionals and schools throughout the New York tri-state area. Aside from her private practice, Norma and the Smart Parenting experts offer seminars and customized lectures to teachers and parents at schools, corporations and non for profit organizations.

Norma is the Co-Founder and Clinical Director of The Rockland Institute for Psychotherapy. The Rockland Institute is an OASAS Approved School for Addiction Studies.

In addition, Norma Ross is the President of The International University for Graduate Studies, which offers doctoral degrees to Post Masters-level students. The school specializes in helping students with various degrees from different schools create customized doctoral degrees.

Norma holds a Bachelor's in Commerce and a Master of Science in Education with a concentration in Guidance and Counseling. She has also earned her Doctorate in Psychoanalysis. She has been on The Board of Trustees of The National Association for Advancement of Psychoanalysis (NAAP), and is currently a member of NAAP, the American Counseling Association, and serves as a site visitor and sits on the committee for the American Board for Accreditation in Psychoanalysis.